BODMIN MOOR

BRITISH TOPOGRAPHICAL SERIES

published

Beyond the Great Glen

in preparation

The Chilterns
Fenland Country
The Peak District

BODMIN MOOR

by *E. C. AXFORD*

DAVID & CHARLES

NEWTON ABBOT   LONDON

NORTH POMFRET (VT)   VANCOUVER

To Roger and Mary

ISBN 0 7153 6943 1
Library of Congress Catalog Card Number 75-26357

© E. C. AXFORD 1975

Set in 11 on 13pt Baskerville and printed in
Great Britain by Latimer Trend & Company
Ltd Plymouth for David & Charles (Holdings)
Limited   South Devon House   Newton Abbot
Devon

Published in the United States of America by
David & Charles Inc North Pomfret Vermont
05053 USA

Published in Canada by Douglas David &
Charles Limited   132 Philip Avenue   North
Vancouver BC

CONTENTS

LIST OF ILLUSTRATIONS

LIST OF ILLUSTRATIONS

1   A PROFILE OF THE MOOR

ON a clear day the traveller to the South West has his first view of Bodmin Moor as he reaches the summit of the long hill on the western side of Okehampton. From this point the moor is twenty miles away and he may well feel that the distant hills are not particularly impressive. But as he draws nearer he will realise that he is approaching an area of great interest. It has the quality of individuality and variety of profile that characterise all granite country. He sees the fan-like frieze of the rock row that crowns the long summit of Kilmar, the bold outlines of the crags of Hawk's Tor above the Trebartha woods and the smooth rolling downs of East Moor and Carne Down. As he enters the moor and ascends to Cannaframe the majestic slopes of Brown Willy rise into view, with the rock castles of Roughtor peering over its shoulder. If he turns aside to examine the country more closely he will find that the open moorland is invaded by large parcels of enclosed land which reach in to almost every part, and the area is criss-crossed with narrow lanes. It is a wilderness in miniature, full of contrasts. From the well-known Jamaica Inn, with its car-park crowded to the limit in the high holiday season, it is only a mile to Dozmary Pool, that quiet tarn on its hilltop, reflecting the empty sky. From the open moor beside the pool he can look across the hidden valley of the Fowey to the strikingly placed prehistoric stone circle of Goodaver. In the other direction is a rolling country dotted with isolated farm-houses. Here and there the undulating downs are punctuated by hills, every one of them different: Brown Gelly with its barrow field on the summit, Hawk's Tor in Blisland parish, another circular knoll crowned by a mass of boulders, Catshole Tor, a tumble of rocks that leans out towards the long flank of Brown Willy. The lanes wind here and there, linking the farms. There can be no place on the moor that is more than a couple of miles from the nearest motorable road.

The scale is minute. The highest hill attains a mere 1,375ft (420 metres on the new map); the moor measures only ten miles each way but it conveys a sense of loneliness and isolation quite out of proportion to its size and until recent years those who lived on it were in a world of their own. When my father was fishing on the upper Delank in the autumn of 1914 he came across a farmer who was quite unaware that we had been at war with Germany for over two months. Perhaps it was the same farmer who said to C. Lewis Hind, the author of *Days in Cornwall* (1907), ''Tis lucky the doctor's a huntin' man or he'd never find Garrow'. The house this man occupied is almost certainly derelict today but if it is still inhabited it will probably have television or at least a radio to keep its owner abreast of current affairs. But though Bodmin Moor is now in contact with the media it still remains inviolate. The walker in this strange, forgotten country, though he is only a mile or so away from the lines of hurtling traffic, will find that he has escaped into a new dimension, into a solitude and peace that defy the close proximity of the contemporary world.

It is the smallness of the scale that is largely responsible for this. A great variety of scene can be experienced in the shortest of walks. One can circumnavigate Roughtor in less than an hour and the hill presents a different profile every minute. From the south it seems a somewhat ungainly mass; from the west it is a nobly proportioned mountain. The sugar-loaf appearance of Brown Willy as you see it from Davidstow Moor, conveys no hint of its long multi-peaked crest which is visible from the higher reaches of the Delank valley less than a mile away. Kilmar, the highest of the hills on the eastern flank of the moor, is an insignificant pile of rocks as you approach it from Henwood across Langstone Downs, but if you come to it from the other

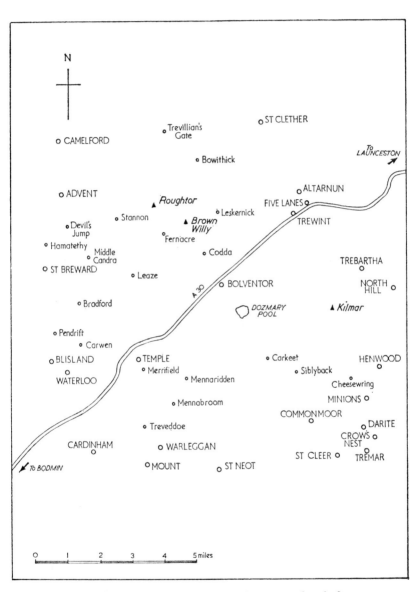

N

o CAMELFORD

o Trevillian's Gate

o ST CLETHER

o Bowithick

To LAUNCESTON

o ADVENT

▲ Roughtor

o Stannon

o Leskernick

o ALTARNUN

FIVE LANES o

o Devil's Jump

▲ Brown Willy

o Fernacre

TREWINT

o Hamatethy

o Middle Candra

o ST BREWARD

o Codda

TREBARTHA

o Leaze

A 30

o BOLVENTOR

NORTH HILL o

o Bradford

DOZMARY POOL

▲ Kilmar

o Pendrift

o Carwen

o BLISLAND

o WATERLOO

o TEMPLE

o Merrifield

o Carkeet

o Siblyback

HENWOOD o

o Mennaridden

Cheesewring

MINIONS o

o Mennabroom

COMMONMOOR o

o Treveddoe

o DARITE

CROWS NEST o

TREMAR

CARDINHAM o

To BODMIN

o WARLEGGAN

ST CLEER o

o MOUNT

o ST NEOT

0   1   2   3   4   5 miles

Bodmin Moor, showing the principal settlements and main features side the difference is miraculous. It towers above Trewartha farm-house like an advancing army terrible with banners.

It is not only the tors that exert fascination. The smooth rolling downs have their atmosphere too and, like the tors, they seem bigger than they actually are. To the walker, East Moor, the open stretch of country between Fox Tor and Carey Tor in the moor's north eastern corner, can seem a vast wilderness though there is little more than a square mile of it. You may come across it in high summer when the distant view is lost in shimmering heat, or on squelching wet days when the rain-clouds roll in from Boscastle and empty themselves on Carne Down or Hendra Beacon and it is difficult to believe that the long loads are thundering up the slope to Cannaframe only a mile away and that you are only a ten-minute walk from the moor's edge. Even the smallest expanses of down, like Shallow Water Common to the north of the A30 or Letter Moor or Penkestle Moor in St Neot, convey a sense of magnitude out of all proportion to their actual size. In mist or driving rain one is always conscious of immensities of distance beyond the limit of one's restricted vision; on clear sunny days the quality of the light magnifies every natural feature.

Whatever the weather, the sense of loneliness and antiquity is persistent: all over the moor's surface are relics of ancient man, the stone circles, the hut settlements that date from the Bronze Age, the hill forts of our Celtic ancestors, the abandoned workings of the tin streamers and the derelict farm-houses which were occupied little more than a generation ago. All these things are not only of interest to the archaeologist, they contribute to the individual atmosphere which gives this country its distinctiveness.

This is a granite area—and granite is curious stuff. You come up to it through the tangle of woodlands that clothe the river valleys around the moor and you feel like a diver breaking surface into sunlight. As you emerge onto it you become aware that beneath the skin of the earth there is a life which uplifts the spirit. You feel this in all the granite areas of the South

West: on Dartmoor; even on Hensbarrow, though the natural landscape has been almost obliterated by the china-clay industry; on Carnmenellis where the land has been superficially changed by the miner and the quarrier; and very strongly indeed in the haunting hill country west of St Ives.

Small though it is, the moor exhibits a considerable variety of scene. From the west it is dominated, as indeed is the whole countryside from the high land north of Boscastle to the estuary of the Camel, by Roughtor and Brown Willy, Cornwall's highest hills. These beautifully proportioned tors take the eye from dozens of viewpoints in the coastal parishes. They can be seen from every field gateway that borders the road from St Endellion to Delabole; you even get a satisfying glimpse of them, almost at sea-level, from the pretty eighteenth-century Trewornan Bridge which spans the Amble river just before it enters the estuary of the Camel. Here on the west, the boundary of the moor is washed by the Camel, the only sizeable Cornish stream which empties into the Atlantic. It has two tributaries on the eastern side, the Delank and the Henon river. These, like all the moorland streams, rise in indeterminate boggy tracts and move placidly from one peat-stained pool to the next in a gradual descent to the moor's edge, from which they tumble rapidly down to the softer country below. The Delank is typical. It rises at 1,000ft in Roughtor Marsh and after following its course for some five miles it flows under Delphy Bridge, which is only 300ft below its source. It then rushes down through the gorge of Hantergantick to join the Camel at a point which is only two miles from Delphy Bridge and 500ft below. As one views the moor from the west the dramatic descent of the Delank is hidden by the high land around Penpont, because it approaches the Camel in a south-westerly direction. The Henon tributary makes a more obviously spectacular approach to the main stream. This river also rises at 1,000ft and follows a south-westerly course under Roughtor. It then turns sharply north-east and enters a narrow gorge above Trecarne, guarded by two great rock castles, one on either side of the valley, known as the Devil's Jump, because, when the devil was driven out of Cornwall by the Celtic saints, he crossed the gorge by leaping from one rock to the other.

The northern fringe of the moor looks bleak and inhospitable. This high plateau conveys a sense of dereliction because of the abandoned aerodrome with its ruined sheds and its acres of weed-covered runways. East of Roughtor and Brown Willy the moor is flanked by a number of rounded hills, High Moor, Buttern Hill and Bray Down. There are no villages here and very few houses. But although it seems aloof and forbidding, access to the moor on foot is easier from the north than from any other quarter. From Trevillian's Gate on the Camelford-Altarnun Road you can step straight onto open country and walk past Lanlavery Rock to Showery Tor and the summit of Roughtor, and from Bowithick, a small settlement which lies on a loop road, it is easy to make your way up into the hills. Beyond Bowithick the loop road runs through unfenced land at the moor's foot to West Carne and Altarnun and you can leave it to climb Bray Down and sample the considerable stretch of open country which includes Leskernick Hill and Hendra Beacon. This part of the moor is scarred by mine workings both ancient and recent, for wolfram has been taken here in modern times. The hills are empty; there are no moor-land houses north of the upper valley of the Fowey except Cannaglaze, on the eastern slopes of Bray Down, and Lesker-nick close to the river, although there is much evidence of past occupation for there are considerable numbers of Bronze Age settlements.

The Inney, the chief Cornish tributary of the Tamar, is the guardian of the moor on its northern side until its duties are taken over by the Penpont Water. The two headwaters of this stream rise in the bogs on either side of Buttern Hill and tumble down for a couple of hundred feet to Bowithick. Here the streams unite and turn eastward to run along the edge of the moor through Altarnun to join the main stream at Two Bridges, where the A30 crosses the rivers just before their confluence.

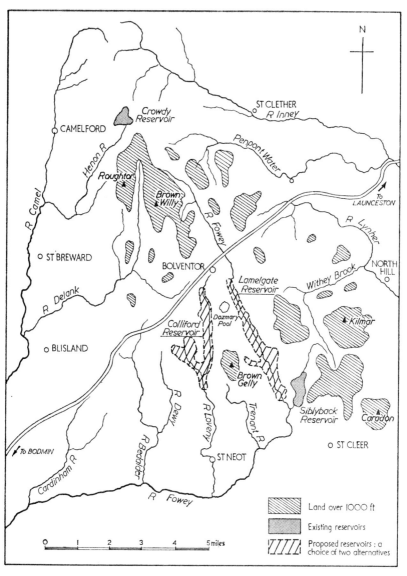

Bodmin Moor's rivers and their tributaries and sites of reservoirs

The eastern side has its guardian river too. This is the Lynher (from 'Lyn-hir', or Long Lake) which runs beside the moor as far as Bathpool. The hills that line this side are a varied and impressive array. Ridge, in the north, is smooth and rounded. Next to it, in vigorous contrast, is Hawk's Tor which stands proudly above the woods of Trebartha like a Norman keep. Between these two hills is the valley of the Witheybrook, 'most beautiful of Cornish burns' as Henderson calls it. The Witheybrook rises under Stowe's Hill and flows northwards under Smallacoombe Downs. At Rushyford Gate it turns to the east and runs off the moor through Trebartha, tumbling down 400ft in less than a mile over a series of delightful cascades. Beyond Hawk's Tor is Kilmar which, next to Roughtor, is the most impressive of the Cornish tors. Further south is Bearah Tor and then Sharp Tor, poised over the village of Henwood like a miniature Matterhorn. Then comes Stowe's Hill, crowned with its Iron Age camp and, finally, the great whaleback of Caradon which buttresses the moor against the tumbled land to the south. The eastern profile of the moor lacks the arresting qualities of the view of Roughtor, with the long sloping ridge of Brown Willy behind it as seen from the west, but it is a noble and varied rampart of great attractiveness.

The southern edge of the moor is also bounded by a river, the Fowey itself. This rises as Leland tells us 'in a very wagmore in the side of an Hil'. The hill is Brown Willy and at one time the source of the river was marked by a chapel of St Peter of Fawe, though no trace of the building remains. The river runs through the heart of the moor and follows a straight course in a south-south-easterly direction to Draynes Bridge where it bends to the west and descends by a series of rapids, known as Golitha Falls, through the woodlands of Trenant and Treverbyn. Soon after passing under the fifteenth-century Treverbyn Bridge the river enters the beautiful Glynn valley and forms the southern boundary of the parishes of St Neot, Warleggan and Cardinham, the loveliest part of inland Cornwall.

For about nine miles, a third of its length before it reaches

Page 17 (above) Roughtor and Brown Willy: a typical moorland view. Note the shelter belt of conifers, the new road to Middle Candra and the intake with open moor beyond; *(below)* Middlemoor Cross, standing bleak and exposed, is the most remote cross on the moor

Page 18 (above) Slades is typical of empty farm-houses abandoned with the old subsistence farming. It stands under Roughtor, two miles from the nearest metalled road; *(below)* Dozmary Pool. This lovely tarn, a mile in circumference, stands at 900ft. The view is to the south, with Brown Gelly in the distance

the tidal estuary, the Fowey is a moorland river which used to give its name to the whole area. In the thirteenth-century when the mining districts of the west were divided into provinces, or stannaries, the moorland region between Launceston and Bodmin was known as Fowey-Moor. There are many who think that this name should have been retained, for, as Charles Henderson has said, 'The Devonians have not behaved so ungenerously to their Dart as to change the name of Dartmoor but the Cornish have changed the name of Fowey-Moor to the meaningless Bodmin Moor'.

All along the south, the edge of the moor merges almost imperceptibly with the adjoining country. The hills here are lower and none of them attains a height of 1,000ft. The patches of intake are more numerous and there are several areas of open down like St Cleer Common, Goonzion in St Neot and Treslea in Cardinham which reach out towards the enclosed country and have a considerable area of fenced land behind them. Perhaps the most attractive feature of the southern sector of the moor is the incidence of narrow, well-wooded valleys through which a number of delightful trout streams thread their way down to the Fowey in the main valley below. There is the unnamed stream which comes down from Whitebarrow Downs past the farm-house of Trenant (the Cornish name means the settlement in the valley), and a mile farther to the west is the much larger river, the Loveny (pronounced *Love-enny*) which waters the parish of St Neot. The Ordnance Survey map rather unenterprisingly calls it the St Neot River but the pretty name, Loveny, was given to it at least as far back as the thirteenth-century. Local people still know it by this name which, in recent years, was given to one of the village streets and the name has also been adopted by a male voice choir in the district. It is to be hoped that in the interests of both euphony and accuracy, the next edition of the Ordnance Survey map will restore to this charming little river its ancient name.

Farther to the west is another tributary of the Fowey which is marked on the map as the Warleggan river. This river rises high on the moor close to Hawk's Tor in Blisland parish. It passes below the hamlet of Temple and runs due south past the western flank of Carburrow Tor. Henderson tells us that a Charter of 1291 in the *Launceston Cartulary* names it Medaldhur, very like the Cornish word 'Medhalder' which means sweetness, but this may be a coincidence for the last syllable looks like 'dour' which means water. It was called Bedalder in the seventeenth-century and the name is still used locally. Towards the end of its course it is joined by its own tributary, the Dewy, a pretty stream that washes the eastern side of Carburrow. This ancient name survives in several local place names: Deweymeads, a moorland farm not far from its source, Castle Dewy a little farther south and, farther on again, on the St Neot side of the valley there is an ancient house, Lantewey, a name which is probably a variant of Nant Dewy. The stream runs over dark shale as it approaches the Bedalder and this may account for its name as 'dhu' is Cornish for black. Spanning the Bedalder river are two interesting bridges. High on the moors under Blacktor Downs, the old turnpike from Bolventor to Temple crosses the river and here there is a bridge dating from the eighteenth-century when the road was constructed. Beside it is a paved causeway which dates from much earlier times. Just below the confluence of the Dewy and the Bedalder is Panters Bridge, a beautiful bridge of the early fifteenth-century very like Treverbyn. This carried the main road from Liskeard to Bodmin through St Neot, a road now superseded by the A38. Panters Bridge was called Pontwise Bridge in the seventeenth-century and may well be the Pontiesu (Jesus Bridge) referred to in a charter of 1241. If so, the reference would be to an earlier bridge replaced by the present fifteenth-century structure. The bridge which is only 8½ft wide is unsuitable for modern traffic and a well designed and attractive modern bridge now carries the roadway. The county council has used the old bridge as a lay-by, surely one of the most attractive in Cornwall, and it is still possible to drive over it.

Half a mile farther to the west a small stream comes down

past Cabilla Wood through a narrow valley and farther to the west again another unnamed river runs through the parish of Cardinham to enter the Fowey not far from the fine Regency mansion of Glynn. All these streams come off the moor through narrow wooded gorges above which stand the naked tors, making the most of their insignificant height: Berry Down in St Neot, Carburrow in Warleggan, St Bellarmin's Tor and Colvannick in Cardinham. Beneath them the old main road follows its switchback way through the unspoilt countryside, an area rich in memorials of the past—Iron Age camps, holy wells, inscribed stones and ancient crosses. It is a quiet attractive country, always aware of the moor just over its shoulder, a mixture of richness and austerity, of luxuriant sheltered valleys and high windswept downs.

Bodmin Moor boasts no high hills: there are only two that exceed 1,300ft and another four that reach the 1,200ft mark. All these hills, with the exception of Brown Willy and Hendra Beacon stand on the moor's edge and there are no large-scale features in the centre. The middle of the moor is given over to rolling downs varied by occasional outcrops of rock and a considerable number of boggy regions, the sources of the moorland streams. Because of its lower altitude the moor has little of the blanket bog so frequently found on Dartmoor, but there are numerous 'pisky pits', bright green areas amongst the tussocks of rough grass and cotton grass, which are easily detected and best avoided. In *A Book of Cornwall* (1899), the Reverend S. Baring-Gould describes how he nearly lost his life in one of these bogs:

> All at once I sank above my waist and was being sucked further down. I cried to my companion but in the darkness he could not see me. The water finally reached my armpits. Happily I had a stout bamboo, some six feet long, and I placed this athwart the surface and held it with my arms as far expanded as possible. By jerks I gradually succeeded in lifting myself and throwing my body forward till finally I was able to cast myself full length upon the surface. The suction had been so great as to tear the leather gaiters I wore off my legs. I lay full length gasping for

nearly a quarter of an hour before I had breath and strength to advance and then wormed myself along on my breast until I reached dry land.

Every topographical writer who deals with Bodmin Moor mentions the bogs, but although these are numerous and some even dangerous, there is, in this quiet and open country, plenty of firm and high ground to walk on. Walking or riding the moor is a delight at any time of the year. In summer, when most visitors come, it presents a picture of every imaginable shade of green. In autumn when the bracken begins to turn and the moor grasses follow suit, every hillside and plateau glows with a rich bronze colour against which the dwarf oaks and the thorn bushes, stripped of their leaves by the equinoctial gales, stand black in contrast. Gradually the colours fade. The land becomes sere and bare, a dun waste. It is 'the shaven moor' as A. L. Rowse calls it in 'Home-coming to Cornwall: December, 1942', a moving personal poem in which the scene is closely and exactly described. Away from the moor inland Cornwall is honeycombed with deep, sheltered valleys, choked with luxuriant growth throughout the year. In the lowlands winter is easily forgotten, but not on the high downs where the bones of the land are laid bare. There is always a wind blowing to drive the clouds across the wide expanse of sky and provide an ever-changing shadow pattern which lends variety to the bleached surface of the moor. It seems that every time you lift your eyes the winter landscape of the moor is different. Spring comes late to these uplands. It is not till May that the bracken shoots thrust up their pale green shepherds' crooks through the grey turf to join the sparse covering of grass. The surface of the moor does not become verdant again until summer has enriched the valleys and then once more there is a patchwork quilt of every shade of green.

Except in the bleak northern area there are houses all over the moor. In Bronze Age times when the climate was better than it is today the moor carried a heavy population. The Domesday Book records very little occupation of this somewhat infertile region, but resettlement soon began. The Templars arrived during the twelfth-century and Merrifield Farm, quite near their settlement, was recorded in 1241. Fernacre, between Brown Willy and Roughtor and perhaps the most isolated place of human occupation on the moor, was mentioned in 1327. Maidenwell on the edge of Cardinham Moor is another fourteenth-century settlement. The most recent edition of the one-inch Ordnance Survey map names over 100 moorland farm houses and there are many more that the map does not indicate. Though Bodmin Moor has a superficial resemblance to Dartmoor it is really very different, largely because it is at a lower altitude. It is more comfortable to live in. But the days of small farms are over and many of the moorland houses have been empty for several decades. Some of them stand far from metalled roads. Butter's Tor farm-house, two miles from the nearest road was abandoned some fifty years ago; Garrowgate, under Roughtor, has been empty since World War II; Leskernick, more than a mile from the lane that runs from the A30 to Codda, was occupied until the mid-1960s. Some of the abandoned houses are used to shelter stock or store hay, others are gradually disintegrating and sinking back into the moor. Around them are field walls in varying states of repair, some little different from the Bronze Age hedges erected over 3,000 years ago.

Some of the moorland houses are buildings of much the same construction as the byres and shippons that adjoin them, for it was not uncommon for a farmer who had acquired a ninety-nine-year lease on an area of moorland to erect his own dwelling house as a spare time occupation, when he was actually farming the land. Some are ancient buildings of great simplicity and charm. There is Leaze, for instance, a farm-house in the centre of the moor. This was erected in the middle of the seventeenth-century and contains only a tiny room which served as entrance lobby, with the living room beyond it. Over it is a single bedroom. The house, constructed of roughly coursed rubble and great blocks of moorstone, is built into the land and snugly

sheltered from the prevailing wind. After more than 300 years
it still looks solid and secure. Its nearest neighbour, Ivey, is
another seventeenth-century house. Larger houses of similar
date, some with later additions, can be found around the edge
of the moor. There is Trethin in the parish of Advent and in the
southern part of the moor, above the Dewy river, is the charming Mennabroom. Lantewey in the same valley is a large house,
a handsome L-shaped building with well proportioned granite
mullions. Nearly all the moorland houses, in whatever century
they were built, share one characteristic. No matter how exposed they seem to be, it will be found on close examination
that they have been very carefully sited, taking advantage of
some dip or fold in the ground to gain for them a measure of
protection from the wind. One thinks of Codda, an ancient
house almost half-way between Bolventor and Brown Willy,
which clings to the hillside as if it grew there. Or there is
Newton in Blisland parish, for some years the home of Margaret
Leigh who describes her moorland farming life in *Harvest of
the Moor*:

> The homestead is built in a slight hollow sheltered by sloping
> fields from the fury of the south and west. A few trees—ash,
> sycamore and oak—are grouped about the house, and their
> tall wind-vexed branches, strangely contorted and all turned
> away from the sea, are a conspicuous landmark, beside which
> the low granite buildings look small and meaningless, no more
> than boulders strewn upon the surface of the moor.

Maps of the early nineteenth-century show a network of roads
around and across the fringes of the moor, though the centre,
except for the main road through Bolventor, remains inviolate.
Many of the roads shown on these maps can still be seen as
faint grassy tracks and it is probable that they were never much
better, for seventeenth- or eighteenth-century Cornwall did not
enjoy a very high reputation for the quality of its roads.

Celia Fiennes who travelled through Cornwall in 1695 writes
of the many holes and sloughs:

> Wherever there is clay ground, and when by rains they are filled

with water, it is difficult to shun danger. Here my horse was quite down in one of these holes full of water, but by the good hand of God's providence which has always been with me ever a present help in time of need, for giving him a good strap he flounced up again, though he had gotten quite down his head and all.

Later in her account this vigorous and intrepid lady describes how she visited Comblefford (Camelford) 'over steep hills 9 miles more; some of this way was over commons of black moorish ground full of sloughs'. Sixty years later the situation was no better and a correspondent in *The Gentleman's Magazine* writes in 1754: 'Cornwall, I believe at present has the worst roads in all England, a great part of which are intolerable, remaining just in the same rude situation in which the deluge left them.' But the second half of the eighteenth-century brought a great improvement. There were a number of Turnpike Acts to initiate good roads in the West Country and an Act of 1769 provided for a direct route to the west across the middle of the moor. The road followed the line of the present A30 and replaced a bridle path so indeterminate and dangerous that, as we read in the journals of the early Methodist preachers, it was sometimes necessary for a traveller to employ a guide to lead him through these wastes, while medieval travellers made out their wills before attempting the journey. So the road was constructed and it was possible for William Marshall, writing in 1796 to comment: 'The road in general is good. For a considerable way the stones are covered with a kind of rough sand, or small gravel, apparently the loose materials of which granite is composed making an admirable road'. The rough sand to which he refers would be growan, or rab as it is called in Cornwall, an admirable surface for horse-drawn traffic. It was almost at the same date that an unknown writer described the road from Five Lanes to Bodmin as '13 miles of good road over several mountains'.

The moor is now threaded by a number of narrow, but well surfaced lanes, which make their way over the open downs, burying themselves at intervals between high hedges that enclose the intakes. From the A30 four roads run north. One leaves Trewint and another starts just to the east of Bolventor to serve a number of moorland farms. The other two are through roads; the first turns in at Temple crossroads and makes its way past Bradford and over Kerrow Downs to Blisland. A turning to the right on this road crosses the Delank at Delphy Bridge on its way to St Breward. The other road starts at the moor's edge opposite Colvannick Tor and brings you to Blisland too, an attractive, winding lane which crosses Trehudreth Downs and offers delightful views of Blisland churchtown tucked into its hillside.

On the south side of the A30 is the loop road that passes through Temple, following the former course of the turnpike and three other roads which lead to the A38, the main road from Liskeard to Bodmin. One of these crosses Redhill Downs, Letter Moor and Goonzion Downs to the Halfway House, built on the site of an old coaching inn beside the Fowey. Opposite Jamaica Inn is the entrance to the winding lane which goes by Dozmary Pool, along the flank of Brown Gelly and over White-barrow Downs to Wenmouth Cross, just above St Neot. There is another road to the south which starts just beside it and drops down to the valley of the Fowey. It follows the river down past Harrowbridge to Trekievesteps and joins the road from Minions to Doublebois at Redgate. It is marked on the first edition of the Ordnance Survey map and is probably the 'modern road cut across the moor from Jamaica Inn to Liskeard' mentioned in the *Cornwall Register* published in 1847. For most of its course the road runs close beside the river, a delightful route to follow either by car or on foot. This charming valley makes an immediate appeal. It is wild and remote and essentially a moorland area, but at the same time a warm and sheltered place, lapped in by the hills and graced by a number of attractive farm-houses—Trezibbett clinging to the hillside below the stone circle, Ninestones, standing high with a fine view down the valley to the narrow gorge below Lamelgate, and the ancient dwelling of Carkeet under Hill Tor. It is a miniature world of its own, cut off from the surrounding moor and yet a part of it.

Of all this network of roads it is the lane that leads to Dozmary Pool that attracts most attention during the holiday season. Like that geological *tour-de-force*, the Cheesewring, the unexpected upland tarn of Dozmary has drawn sightseers from the earliest times. Leland, Norden and Carew all mention it; Celia Fiennes visited it; on Midsummer Day, 1773, a 'great revel' was held there and according to a report in the *Sherborne Mercury* the owner of the pool charged a parking fee 'of one penny each for horses, those refusing to pay to be charged for trespass'. Carew tells us in *The Survey of Cornwall* that 'the country people held many strange conceits of this pool, as, that it did ebb and flow, that it had a whirlpool in the midst thereof, and that a faggot once thrown thereunto, was taken up at Fowey haven, six miles distant'. Dozmary's legendary associations with King Arthur are probably recent. Older and more typically Cornish is the linking of this weird place with John Tregeagle, the unjust steward who served Lord Robartes of Lanhydrock in the seventeenth century. His restless spirit has to expiate his crimes by baling out the pool with a limpet shell with a hole in the bottom. As he goes about his endless task he is pursued by devils and their shrieking can be heard on any windy night as he flees across the moor for sanctuary at the chapel of Roche Rocks at the other side of Bodmin. There is a taste of the concluding stanzas of Widecombe Fair in this story, but legends about Dozmary, courtly or bucolic, are only to be expected. It is a queer place, full of 'atmosphere'. The country people used to think it was bottomless. Leland, more matter-of-fact but almost as inaccurate, says that it is fifteen fathoms deep 'by estimation'. In point of fact you can wade across it at almost any time. It is a shallow, diamond-shaped pool about a mile in circumference, surrounded by rough fields and it stands high on the moor in a shallow saucer of land. The sudden and unexpected view of it as you approach it from Bolventor or Wenmouth Cross is breath-taking. It is one of the strangest things in this very strange country.

Charles Henderson mentions a reference in a charter of 1239 in the *Launceston Cartulary* to a *magnum iter plaustorum* or 'great road of wagons' which led from the Chapel of St Peter of Fawe at the source of the Fowey to 'Stingede-lace' (Stimgoid Lake). Could the lake be Dozmary? A track can still be followed from close to the river's source past Leskernick and over Scaddick Hill to a ford on the upper Fowey, and up to the shoulder of Tolborough Tor near Black Hill. Here it becomes a metalled road and runs to Bolventor. From this point there is a choice of ways to Dozmary, down to St Luke's and up over the hill to the lake or by the existing road which was only a rough track forty years ago. But however you make your way from Brown Willy to Dozmary it is hard to believe that you could be following the route of a 'great road of wagons'. This area must always have been a wild and lonely place for it is so still in spite of the cars parked thickly in front of Jamaica Inn and the trunk road that runs past it. Dozmary is a quiet place that preserves its secrets.

In Leland's day the moor around Dozmary Pool was the home of the red deer, 'the which when they be schafed, take the sayde Poole for Soyle'. But the deer are back again. Some have moved down from Exmoor to the Trebartha woods but they are few in number and not often seen. But on Bodmin Moor, in spite of its limited area, in spite of the busy main road that bisects it, the sense of peace and solitude that it conveys is appreciated by animals as well as humans. It is almost impossible to walk on the moor without seeing a fox and it is said that there are more than 100 living on Brown Willy. This hill is also the home of a large colony of badgers and their setts are numerous all over the area. In spite of periodical attacks of myxomatosis there are also considerable numbers of rabbits on the moor and I recall a drive across Craddock Moor in early summer just after daybreak, when the road was full of them.

It is not only the secluded nature of the region that makes it an attractive area for wildlife study. Within the narrow moorland limits there is a great variety of habitat: open downland, rocky tors, marshes (these are diminishing rapidly because of drainage and land reclamation schemes) river valleys, quarries, ruined buildings and areas of deciduous and coniferous woodland. There are few ponds and lakes in Cornwall and the only sizeable natural sheet of water on the moor is Dozmary, but the reservoirs may also provide a refuge for a wide range of migratory and wintering wildfowl and waders. This will be some compensation for the fact that reservoir development on the moor is objectionable in many other ways.

The bird-watcher finds the moor very rewarding. On the open downs nesting ring ouzel and whinchat are sometimes recorded and these birds do not breed in any other part of Cornwall. The very rare Montagu's harrier is sometimes seen on the moor. This bird will nest in conifer plantations during their period of early growth, but forsakes them when the trees are well grown. Afforestation which developed considerably during the middle years of the present century, though the general appearance of the area has not been improved by it, has rewarded the naturalist. It has been responsible for the first record of breeding redpolls in Cornwall and the only two heronries on the moor are sited in the coniferous woods. The bird-watcher will find the marshlands full of interest. They are the only nesting places in the county for the common snipe, the common redshank and the dunlin. Frogs, now becoming rare in this country, are found in considerable numbers in the marshes. These areas are also the natural habitat of many interesting plants, cotton grass, hare's tail, marsh violets, bog asphodel and some of the insect-catching plants.

Bodmin Moor is of great value to the botanist and the zoologist, but because of the pressures on the area (these will be discussed at length in the last chapter) both the fauna and flora are likely to be seriously affected, particularly the latter. Radical changes are likely to take place not only in the moor itself but in the indigenous plant and animal life. As we have seen, afforestation has created new habitats for bird life, but there is more loss than gain for as the plantings mature, the underlying vegetation is almost completely destroyed. The drowning of river valleys on the granite by the construction of reservoirs obliterates marshy ground and the wealth of flora it supports. The improvement of hill pasture is inimical to moorland plant life and substitutes for it a kind of herbage similar to that provided by lowland pasture. The overgrazing of some parts of the downs destroys the conditions in which many species of birds and insects flourish. It is because the moor is now so heavily stocked that there is very much less heather than there used to be. The decrease of heather is also the result of the practice of swaling, of burning off the gorse and other growth on the downs in the early spring. Swaling is controlled but not always effectively. It improves pasture up to a point, but a good deal of hill land is swaled much too frequently so that bracken tends to replace heather on the downs and checks the growth of other kinds of ground cover. Where these developments do not affect it the vegetational characteristics of the moor are of particular interest and Carolyn Brewster, who has made a detailed study of the region, has added a note on this subject to this chapter.

Here and there in this island there are small areas of countryside—one thinks of Otmoor in Oxfordshire, or Holderness, or the Norfolk salt marshes, or, in spite of the encroaching urbanisation, of the forest of Charnwood—which exert an inexplicable power and fascination; Bodmin Moor is one of these.

VEGETATIONAL CHARACTERISTICS OF THE MOOR

Carolyn Brewster

The characteristics of moorland vegetation are the result of long and complicated natural processes of development and degeneration, as well as the impact made by man's land-usage over many centuries. In general terms the typical plant associations of Bodmin Moor can be divided into grasslands, boglands and woodlands. The high-level heather moor which might have been expected from the topographical situation and the facies of the area, and which once was more widespread, is now restricted to several isolated locations in the south eastern corner of the moor, where it is perpetuated by the absence of grazing. The dominant plant in this community is ling, associated with the bent and fescue grass, bell heather, bilberry and gorse or furze.

By far the most widespread of the plant communities on the moor is that of the grasslands which can be divided into the grass moor proper and the bent-fescue association. The true grass moor is widely developed over the damper parts of the moor and is dominated by the purple moor grass. Mat grass, often characteristic of this grassland type in other similar areas of Great Britain, is restricted on Bodmin Moor because of the diversity of grazing stock. The grasses which characterise the bent-fescue association are the common bent together with velvet and bristle-leaved bent as well as red and sheep's fescue. Intermingled in these communities, which occur on the drier and less peaty soils, are the heath grass, heath bedstraw and tormentil.

It is characteristic of Bodmin Moor that its grasslands are composed of scattered societies which are made up of mixtures or mosaics of the grasses and other species including ling, furze, bracken and rushes, the actual pattern being very much dependant on man, and his grazing and management techniques. The history of furze on the moor is somewhat obscure; the western gorse (*Ulex gallii*) has almost certainly been present as in France and Wales from distant times, but the common gorse (*Ulex europaeus*) so useful as grazing for stock, was possibly introduced into Cornwall from Ireland in the eighteenth century, as it is thought to have been in North and mid-Wales. One of the effects of swaling the gorse, still used as a management technique on the moor, is to create a new flush of growth for grazing. Bracken, a significant feature of the vegetation of other hill areas, is restricted on Bodmin Moor in a general way to the clitter (a pile of loose rocks) slopes and tors, but may occur on other dry sites where grazing is restricted.

Conditions suitable for bog growth are found in the relatively shallow valleys on the granite uplands. There is evidence that sometime after 500 BC these were much more extensively developed, the area of this extension being marked today by a thin layer of native hill peat. The vegetation of the valley bogs is richly diversified; the bog mosses are more extensively developed on Bodmin Moor than in most other areas of Cornwall. However, when compared with the Irish boglands, the sphagnum community in the South West is very restricted because of disturbance by man over many centuries whilst streaming for tin, and by burning as a vegetational management technique. Along with the bog mosses in this habitat are combinations of purple moor grass, white-beaked sedge, cotton grass and deer grass, some of which provide a reasonably good feed for the grazing stock.

These valley bogs are of outstanding botanical interest because they provide a habitat for several rare species: the pale butterwort, the common and long-leaved sundews, the marsh violet, the bog asphodel, the bog bean, the ivy-leaved bell flower, the heath spotted orchid and the very rare and restricted tiny yellow bog orchid. Here, too, grows the heath grass, mostly confined to wetter areas, the localised heath rush surprisingly rich in calcium, and the very conspicuous soft and compact rushes. All these are intermingled on occasions with cross-leaved heath, ling and several species of sedge. In a few places such as Witheybrook Marsh and Dozmary Pool the bog may still be seen to be developing, but this diverse habitat is more vulnerable than most by reason of the ever-present temptation to commoners to cut drainage ditches and so lower the water-table. The lakes so often associated with boglands in other regions are represented on Bodmin Moor only by Dozmary Pool which seems to have been an area of continuously open water since late glacial times. Here can still be found the very rare and relict small quillwort.

There is considerable evidence that formerly woodland was far more extensively developed within the area of the moor, although the higher tors have probably been free of trees since the penultimate interglacial. Today the remains of such woodlands may be found in the willow scrub developed along some of the valley bottoms; characteristically, these trees are covered with a dense growth of lichens and particularly *Usnea articulata*, which hangs down with a matted grey-green sausage-shaped thallus. Interesting too are the occasional stunted specimens of hawthorn and holly growing amongst the tor and clitter slopes. In the steep-sided valleys of the granite on the margins of the moor, which have always discouraged the agriculturalist, can be found oak woodlands. Two species of oak occur here, common and sessile, together with various hybrids. Ash, beech, sycamore, hazel and holly provide woodland diversity and are partly responsible for the pleasantly varied ground cover; among the species represented are wood-sorrel, sanicle, bilberry, bramble, honeysuckle, bracken and hard fern. Here too are interesting bryophite communities enriched with rarer species of mosses and liverworts. The rare Tunbridge and Wilson's filmy ferns can be found amongst dark damp boulders on some of the higher tors, the Tunbridge species being found also on boulders in the shade of these valley oak woodlands.

Coniferous plantations have been a feature of the moor since the turn of the last century. The Forestry Commission began large-scale afforestation schemes all over the country during the early 1920s and the main areas on Bodmin Moor were planted between 1928 and 1965. More recently, private timber-growing organisations have bought and planted large acreages of moorland around Smallacoombe Downs. The moorland plantations consist of Sitka spruce with some Lodgepole pine, which have an aspect of unrelieved funereal gloom. In the early stages these forests have a varied ground flora, but as the trees develop, the reduced light and increased quantities of acidic leaf litter cause a rapid impoverishment of the vegetation. The plantings in the river valleys on the margins of the moor

33

have replaced the native oak with a mixture of Douglas fir, Norway spruce and Japanese larch.

No vegetational complex can be understood without reference to the history of its development. On Bodmin Moor the maximum extension of woodland was in the period 5000 to 2500 BC; oak together with some lime, ash and elm grew on the more sheltered hillsides, birch, willow and alder in the valleys, whilst an oak and hazel scrub probably characterised the more exposed hillsides. With the subsequent climatic recessions, these woodlands were reduced by the growth of bogs which formed valley and blanket peat. Many activities of men over the centuries have reduced the woodland areas to their present comparatively diminished dimensions. Such woodlands provided fuel for the inhabitants, charcoal for the tin streamers, and the wherewithal by which the penalised Royalists might pay the heavy fines demanded of them.

Page 35 (above) Kilmar: the long ridge of the tor is crested by rock formations similar to these: *(below)* Roughtor Ford: just beyond the cattle are the field walls of a Bronze Age settlement

Page 36 (above) Rock formations on Carbilly Tor; this natural rock pile, visible from St Breward to Temple, reveals the erosion of the granite into rectangular blocks; *(below)* Trethevy Quoit: the view from the east which shows the antechamber with the opening to the burial chamber beyond; note the hole in the capstone

2 THE TORS

THE story of Bodmin Moor begins some 270 million years ago in Permo-Carboniferous times. This was an age of violent earth movement when the sedimentary rocks laid down in the Devonian and Carboniferous Ages were raised and folded into a mountain range, which stretched from what is now the south-western peninsula, through Brittany and on to the Hartz Mountains in Germany. At this unsettled period in the earth's history a contributory factor in the raising of these mountains was a series of deep-seated bathylithic injections of magma which thrust their way into the sedimentary rocks and, as they cooled, formed large crystals of quartz and feldspar, micas and other minerals. The softer sedimentaries which covered these intrusions have long since been eroded, exposing the granite of Dartmoor, Bodmin Moor, Hensbarrow, Carnmenellis, West Penwith and the Isles of Scilly. The granite is also exposed in smaller isolated areas like Hingston Down, Castle-an-Dinas and St Agnes Beacon which indicates that granites underlie virtually the whole of the south-western peninsula.

The granites vary considerably in texture and in composition because the intrusion of the molten masses of which they are made occurred at different periods in history and because some cooled more rapidly than others. Rapid cooling naturally took place in areas where the magma came into contact with the sedimentary rocks, and the finer texture of granites near the edge of the moor is the result of rapid crystallisation. Some finer granites are found, however, near the centre of the area, close to Dozmary Pool and these are probably the result of later and more acid intrusions.

C

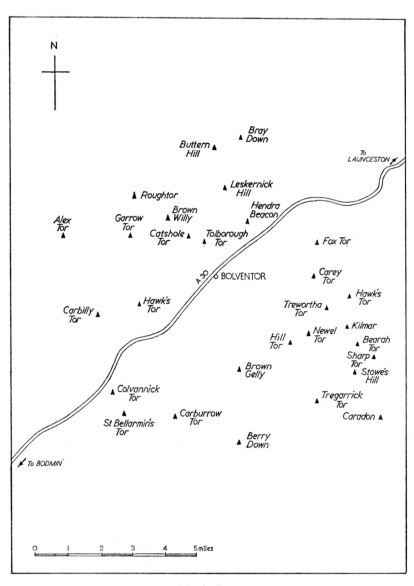

N

Bray
Down ▲

Buttern ▲
Hill

To
LAUNCESTON ↗

Leskernick ▲
Hill

▲ Roughtor

Hendra
Beacon ▲

Alex
Tor ▲

Garrow
Tor ▲

Brown
▲ Willy

Catshole ▲
Tor

Tolborough
▲ Tor

▲ Fox Tor

A 30 ○ BOLVENTOR

Carey ▲
Tor

Carbilly ▲
Tor

▲ Hawk's
Tor

Trewortha ▲
Tor

Hawk's ▲
Tor

▲ Kilmar

Hill ▲
Tor

Newel ▲
Tor

▲ Bearah
Tor

Sharp ▲
Tor

▲ Stowe's
Hill

Colvannick ▲
Tor

▲ Brown
Gelly

Tregarrick ▲
Tor

St Bellarmin's ▲
Tor

Carburrow ▲
Tor

Caradon ▲

Berry ▲
Down

↙ To BODMIN

0   1   2   3   4   5 miles

Principal tors

The slate, the sedimentary rock known in Cornwall as 'killas', along the edge of the moor has been considerably altered by the intruding granite which baked it and caused mineral changes by the introduction of super-heated steam and various gases. This area, the metamorphic aureole, as a result of the impact of the granite in the molten state, yields a great number of minerals of economic importance: copper, tin, lead, zinc, arsenic and wolfram. As we shall see, mining activity, which has been almost continuous for hundreds of years, is chiefly confined to the moor's edge. The sedimentary rocks that surround the moor, the sand, clay and mud deposited in Carboniferous and Permian times, now form a variety of bedded slates, and all around the moor there are slate quarries of varying quality. Some of them are quite small, used, perhaps, for roofing and slate-hanging the walls of a single house and then abandoned as the better quality slate became exhausted. Granites and slates differ considerably; there is much geological variety and it is this that gives the area its enormous fascination and interest.

Granite is resistant to erosion but its structure causes lines of weakness. Joints, known as the tough way and the cleaving way joints, run roughly at right-angles to each other. They divide the mass into columns often separated by openings several inches wide. Water enters these cracks and attacks the large feldspar crystals, breaking up the surrounding rock and forming a coarse sand or gravel, growan, or a grey-white powder, kaolin. Below the surface the feldspar was decomposed even more thoroughly by uprising gases, so that in the production of china-clay which is derived from kaolinised granite, the deeper kaolin is more economical to mine and often superior in quality. The natural cleavage joints facilitate the work of the granite quarrier. Though granite is such a tough material it is fairly easily split at its points of cleavage. All over the moor you find granite blocks which reveal the chisel marks of the quarrier. In earlier times granite was split by wooden wedges driven in and swollen by water to aid the process of cleavage. Basal joints which run horizontally caused the columnar structure to break down on the surface and resulted in the characteristic rectangular blocks found on many of the tors.

The word 'tor' is loosely used as a synonym for hill but, strictly speaking, the tors are the rock castles which appear on so many of the granite hills. Though the rocky tors occupy a very small part of the moor's surface they dominate the landscape. Norden, writing in Elizabethan times, could say:

> The Inlande mountayns are so crowned with mightie rocks, as he that passeth throwgh the Countrye beholdinge some of theis Rockes afar off, may suppose them to be greate Cyties planted on the hills, wherein *prima facie* ther appeareth the resemblance of towres, howses, chimnies and such like, Crags and Rockes vncouered (as may be thowghte) and left bare-headed at the Vniuersal inundation, whose force searching the verie foundations of the yelding earth, carried with violence heapes thereof togeather, making mountayns of valleys, and of valleys loftie hills.

In addition to the great hill castles that Norden describes it will be noticed that many of the hillsides are covered with clitters. These are the result of peri-glacial conditions. The area did not suffer the Ice Age so it shows none of the characteristics of a glaciated region, but it was near enough to the ice-bound areas to be subject to considerable changes of temperature. It became sodden during the summer months and froze during cold spells. In thaw periods the sludge crept down the sides of the hills and the heavy boulders slid down with it. This was the cause of the heaped rocks on the hill slopes. In some areas— the slopes of Roughtor provide an example—these clitters are found in long lines as they were deposited by the streams of sludge.

The faulting of the Armorican mountains of which the granite formed the core has determined the position of some of the tors. It will be noticed that in some areas the granite hills run in parallel formation. There are some striking examples on the eastern side of the moor where Ridge, Hawk's and Trewortha Tors, Kilmar and Bearah Tor form a series of parallel ridges. The two high masses on the west, Roughtor and its northern extension and Brown Willy, run at right-angles to the eastern hills but parallel with each other. These ridges are the result of the upthrust of granite into cracks formed in the now eroded land mass into which they intruded.

In spite of the spectacular nature of the tors the main characteristic of the moorland landscape is a gently rolling countryside crowned with rounded hills. The weathering of the granite has resulted in the formation of growan which lies in considerable depth over the solid rock beneath and this accounts for the smooth appearance of so much of the area. It will be noted, too, that a great deal of the moor's surface constitutes a plateau from which the tors rise as miniature mountains. An early geological survey by Barrow in 1908 commented on the 1,000ft platform, but surprisingly little work has been done to provide an explanation of the series of platforms at various levels down to the 430ft platform, which is so clearly seen near the coast at Tintagel, and of the general uniformity of the cliffs from Tintagel to the estuary of the Camel. But recent work by Balchin, Wooldridge, Linton and Weller has recognised a highly dissected series of platforms over the surface of the moor. These platforms are each bounded on the seaward-facing edge by bluffs or cliffs, not very high and much eroded, but in many places still distinguishable as faces cutting across hill edges. It is thought that some of these platforms are of marine origin for although no evidence of marine life has been found in the Bodmin Moor area, the platforms seem to be related to platforms of similar height in other parts of England where marine fossils have been found. It is unlikely that fossils will be found in this area because they would long since have been dissolved by the peaty water. Water-worn pebbles have been discovered and this suggests some marine association. The 750ft platform is thought to be sub-aerial but the 1,000ft and 675ft platforms are probably marine. The latter can be traced clearly from Cardinham to Pensilva and it appears again at Hingston Down, the granite outlier near Callington.

The present appearance of the moorland rivers owes much

to the platform formation. Most of these streams rise on the 1,000ft platform in marshy basins and their early course is indeterminate. Because of the resistant nature of the granite they do not cut deeply into it but spread out over its surface, creating wide boggy areas, and they only gather force as they run down from one platform to the next. This is particularly noticeable if one follows the course of the Delank which alternates between long placid reaches as it makes its way through comparatively level marshy stretches, and sudden descents over rocky ground. One of its headwaters rises in a marsh near Stanninghill at 900ft and percolates slowly through a boggy area for nearly two miles before it descends rapidly under Scribble Downs to its confluence with the other principal headwater, which comes down from the marsh between Roughtor and Brown Willy. Soon after the streams unite the Delank moves sedately again over another level plateau under Carkees Tor before it tumbles down through giant boulders to Bedrawle Bridge.

All the moorland rivers gather pace and lose height rapidly as they come off the granite into the killas. The Witheybrook makes a spectacular descent to Trebartha, the Fowey rushes down over Golitha Falls in Draynes Wood and the Loveny runs swiftly through the Tremaddock gorge. The Delank and Henon rivers make their way off the moor through steep and narrow valleys at Hantergantick and the Devil's Jump. The killas is softer than the granite and the moorland streams cut deeply into it. In Trevenna wood, opposite Tremaddock, there is a flood beach 160ft above the present course of the Loveny. At the moor's edge the granite passes under the killas but granite boulders are found in the river beds some distance beyond the point where the granite is submerged.

Granite is a general term which covers a wide range of crystalline igneous rocks. Its differences are demonstrated by a variety of hill profile. There are the long serrated ridges of Bearah Tor, Kilmar, Trewortha and Hawk's Tor on the east, the rounded but rocky Alex Tor in St Breward and Hawk's Tor in Blisland, and there are the smooth, virtually rock-free summits of Buttern Hill, Bray Down, Leskernick, Hendra Beacon and Brown Gelly. On Garrow Tor and Brown Willy the rock masses are more closely knit and their jointing is less noticeable than it is on the tors that cover the summits of Roughtor and Kilmar. Similarly the top of St Bellarmin's Tor has a long, sloping, solid surface similar to the platform found on the summit of Trewint Downs and Colvannick is a mass of boulders.

The tors, small though they are, convey an extraordinary sense of magnitude and may well have caused Norden to use the language of hyperbole when he was describing them. 'Mountains—mighty rocks—like great cities planted on the hills' is ponderous writing for a small matter. But it bears the stamp of the eye-witness, one who has looked on these hills and who has acknowledged their power. The actual heights are minuscule. Brown Willy which attains 1,375ft and Roughtor, 1,311ft, are the two highest hills and both rise from the 1,000ft platform. Kilmar which is just short of 1,300ft rises only 330ft from the dry valley on the northern side and less than 200ft from Langstone Downs on the other. But from certain angles these hills and all the other rocky outcrops look bigger and more significant than they actually are. Those who know the moor will have their favourite lines of approach. Roughtor is at its most impressive from the west and Kilmar from the north-west. Even the smallest of the hills have their arresting moments. The insignificant heights of Mutton's Downs and Berry Down should be approached by way of the narrow lane from St Neot up through Tremaddock. At a turn in the road close to the top one suddenly sees them, wild, savage and impressive, although a field hedge clings to the summit of one of them and neither reaches 1,000ft. Or there is Carburrow, a small, dumpy hill crowned with a couple of loose stone cairns. There is a point on the road which runs beside Redhill Downs to Calloways Water from which this insignificant hillock looks immense, almost frightening. St Bellarmin's Tor in the south-western corner of the moor attains the modest height of 880ft and the tor itself rises on the edge of a plateau that is only about 80ft lower. But your view of it as you move westward along the ridge from the Iron Age camp of Bury Castle makes nonsense of the arithmetic and is tremendously impressive.

It is not only the general profile of the tors which is striking; the individual rocks exert their fascination too. Some of them seem to have the significance of modern sculpture and to be imbued with a life of their own. They seem to be alive, waiting motionless as a wild animal might wait until you have gone away, before resuming the secret activity which you have interrupted. The rocks are piled in such a way that they convey an atmosphere that is grim, almost terrifying. So it is on Hill Tor, a cluster of rocks above the valley of the Fowey, which reminds you immediately of Carn Kenidjack in West Penwith, the Hooting Carn of legend.

Weathering has reduced the points of contact between some of the granite blocks so that they are delicately poised and can be moved almost by a touch. On Louden Hill between Roughtor and Stannon there is a very large rocking stone. There are several smaller ones on Trewortha Tor, near Kilmar. On Pendrift Common, in Blisland there was a stone 'so equally ballanced that the winde will move it, whereof I had true experience, and a man with his little finger easily stirr it', as Norden tells us, but the stone had been thrown down before Maclean wrote his *History of Trigg Minor* in 1873.

The most famous assembly of stones in this area is the Cheesewring, half-way up the western side of Stowe's Hill. This, to quote Norden again, is 'a heape of stones, admirablye depending, wherein nature hath done more at adventure (if a man may so speak) than arte or force can doe by greateste deliberation'. The name, Cheesewring, probably derives from cider making, not from the manufacture of cheeses, for the apple pulp is known locally as cheese and the circular stones of the cider press which can still be seen at many old Cornish farmhouses have some resemblance to the natural boulders piled up at the Cheesewring. Many rock formations of this kind can be found on the tors but in none of them do the topmost stones overhang the supporting rocks so dramatically as at Stowe's Hill. This rock pile must have been even more spectacular in former days than it is now. The blasting of the rock in quarrying operations so disturbed it that a buttress of supporting boulders was erected at its southern end. By 1938 the edge of the quarry had advanced to within a few yards of the Cheesewring and the quarry then closed. This remarkable rock pile has been famous for centuries. Carew refers to it and Thomas Staniforth, in his charming diary which describes a visit to Cornwall in 1800, mentions a visit to it on an October day, 'the morning delightful with a sharp frosty autumn air and fog' when he undertook the considerable journey from Lostwithiel to see this 'wonderful pile of stones . . . but whether the work of nature or not I know not'. Now, during the holiday season, it is constantly visited. The surrounding boulders and the ground between them from which every trace of turf is denuded, shine from the trampling of the hordes of visitors who make their way from the Minions road, past the stone circles of the Hurlers, to climb up to this natural curiosity.

There are a number of other rock formations on the moor of considerable interest. On the southern slopes of Carbilly in Blisland parish is a pile of rocks which looks as if a bit of Stonehenge had strayed into Cornwall. Until you approach it closely it is hard to believe that it is a natural formation. On Pendrift Common in the same parish is an enormous granite boulder known as the Jubilee Rock. It has nothing to do with Queen Victoria though her monogram and the date of her jubilee have since been added. In 1809 a Lieutenant Rogers, son of a local resident, decided to commemorate the fifty years of the reign of George III by carving on the rock the Royal Arms, the figure of Britannia, various coats of arms, emblems of Industry, Agriculture, Plenty and Commerce and other insignia. He also composed some stirring verses which were engraved on a brass plate and attached to the rock, from which the following are taken:

> Britannia, may you still maintain
>   The banner of your rights unfurl'd:
> Your wide dominion of the main,
>   Your favours to a humbled world.
>
> May the best fruits creation yields
>   Increase thy bliss, increase thy stores;
> May Plenty load thy smiling fields
>   And Commerce crown thy happy shores.

The brass plate was removed about 100 years ago. The rock is worth a visit not so much because of Rogers's work which is still plainly visible, but for its immense size and the magnificent view the place affords. From Pendrift Common which stands at 700ft in the south-west corner of the moor you look down into the deep gorge of the Delank as it passes through Hantergantick and away across Bodmin to the high land beyond.

Roughtor, the most interesting of all the Cornish hills and the most accessible, exactly conforms with Norden's description and may well have inspired it for the summit with its 'resemblance to towres, howses, chimnies and such like' would have been plainly visible to him if he travelled to the west by way of Launceston and Camelford, the only road available in his day. There are enormous rock castles at either end of the highest point of the ridge and a smaller one in the centre. From the hill above Advent Church the view presents a beautifully pro-portioned mountain which gives the same sort of aesthetic satis-faction as, for instance, the view of Tryfan in North Wales from the Nant Ffrancon pass.

On the northern and higher rock castle are the foundations of the chapel dedicated to St Michael which stood there in medieval times. St Michael is the patron saint of Cornwall (unless you prefer St Piran). Robert, Count of Mortain, half-brother to William the Conqueror, adopted Michael the Arch-angel as his patron saint and bore his banner at the Battle of Hastings. Cornwall was placed under Robert's jurisdiction after the Conquest and this undoubtedly accounts for the fact that so many Cornish churches are dedicated to St Michael.

46

Most of these are hilltop churches or in isolated situations. The chapels on Rame Head, on Roche Rocks, on the summit of Carn Brea in the far west, and most famous of all, at St Michael's Mount, are all dedicated to the Archangel. So is the parish church of Michaelstow, the parish on the west bank of the Camel quite near Roughtor. This is no hilltop church for it is tucked securely into the side of a hill. Just above it, however, on Hellesbury Beacon are the remains of a chapel said to be dedicated to St Syth, but Henderson thinks that St Michael was once honoured there.

The site of the chapel on Roughtor is plainly visible though nothing of the building remains except a tumble of rocks on the eastern side of the tor. A stone which formed the arch of the doorway was removed in 1836 and placed over the door of the Britannia Inn at Trevillian's Gate on the Camelford–Altarnun road. The house, no longer an inn, still stands and the arch, ornamented with a fleur-de-lis, can still be seen.

Roughtor now belongs to the National Trust and within the foundations of the chapel, where the altar once stood, is a plaque on which is inscribed: 'Roughtor on which this memorial is placed has been given to the nation in memory of those who lost their lives while serving in the 43rd (Wessex) Division in the North-west European campaign, 1944–5.' Because of this and because Roughtor is close to the end of the switchback road which runs in from Camelford, it is constantly visited during the summer months. In fine weather there are always cars standing on the hillside above Roughtor Ford and processions of visitors can be seen toiling up the slope past the Bronze Age settlements and their ruined field walls. But the summit of the hill is so thickly covered with rocks that even when there are 100 people scrambling about amongst them, you have no sense of being in a crowd. The broken nature of the ground, the tangle of rocks prevents this. The cliff castle at the southern end is lower than the point where the chapel was built, but the climb up to it is more difficult and spectacular. From the summit there is a fine view westward and southward extending from Bude

47

Haven to the china-clay pyramids on Hensbarrow and St Agnes Beacon. The eastern view is largely blocked by the great mass of Brown Willy on the other side of the Delank.

It is not only in these days of population explosion and heavy tourism that Roughtor has been popular with visitors. There is a lively account in the West Briton newspaper of a gathering of teetotallers there in the summer of 1843—'long lines of carriages and carts with horses picketed around, groups of booths and marquees, where coffee and more solid refreshments were sold'; but the total abstainers did not have it all their own way, for the account goes on, 'nor were there wanting some few spots where other beverages than those used by the teetotallers might be procured'. The success of this function led to a repeat performance in the following year when, we are told, there was an attendance of some 10,000 people. The 'other beverages' were much in evidence and drunken dancing and singing continued far into the night. In 1844 the western slopes of Roughtor had acquired a macabre interest because of the murder of Charlotte Dymond on 4 April in that year by her fellow servant, Matthew Weeks. This took place close to Roughtor Ford. At the meeting subscriptions towards a memorial were collected and the monument still stands close by the river. Weeks was subsequently hanged at Bodmin Gaol and the event was witnessed by 20,000 people, double the number of the teetotallers and drunken hangers-on who attended the jollification at Roughtor a month before.

Roughtor crowns the highest point of a long ridge which runs northward almost to the edge of Davidstow Moor. If you follow the ridge in this direction you come first to the rocky outcrop known as Little Roughtor where there are the remains of an Iron Age camp. Beyond that again is Showery Tor, capped by a prominent 'cheesewring' formation of piled rocks.

Brown Willy is less visited than Roughtor for it is more remote. You can reach it by footpath from Bolventor or by continuing the walk from the summit of Roughtor across the valley of the Delank. Its rather disrespectful name is a corruption of the Cornish 'Bron ewhella', which means highest hill. The view from the summit is tremendous. The sea is visible on both sides as, indeed, it is from many of the Cornish hills. Dartmoor, Exmoor and the whole area of Bodmin Moor are clearly visible and on clear days it is possible to see the Welsh hills. The granite tors here are less spectacular than those on the summit of Roughtor but the sides of the hill are thickly covered with clitters. Walking here is difficult and the easiest ascent is by the worn path which rises steeply to the summit from the northern end of the hill. The ridge slopes gently down to the south towards Brown Willy Downs, the gradual descent punctuated by a series of craggy tors. From the high coastal ridge to the west of the moor, this long sloping hill serves only as a background for the more dramatic outlines of Roughtor but from the other side it is an impressive mountain in miniature. It looks particularly fine from the A30 at the top of Shallow Water Common Hill close to the turning to Temple.

From the summit you can see that on Bodmin Moor, as on Dartmoor, the hills in the centre have rounded summits and few rocky outcrops. The hills here may represent a later intrusion of the granite than that of the rugged tors and are of a different composition. To the north-east are the bare slopes of Leskernick and Hendra Beacon; a little further south is the barrow-crowned Tolborough or Tober Tor, another rounded hill with Catshole Tor a little nearer at hand on an extension of the ridge of which Tolborough is the highest point. Catshole, unlike most of the central hills has some rocky outcrops and piles of clitter beneath. Further away on the other side of Dozmary is Brown Gelly. Its smooth top is crowned by a series of barrows, five of them in a row. The view from Brown Willy to the south-east reveals a wide expanse of rolling downs, Pridacoombe, Butterstor, Shallow Water and Brockabarrow Common, an open lonely country. The traffic on the trunk road which skirts the downland is less than three miles away and is plainly visible, but does little to destroy the sense of remoteness.

On the eastern side of the moor there is a fine complex of

hills, Kilmar, Trewortha, Hawk's and Sharp Tor. They stand in an area known as Twelve Men's Moor of which Henderson says, 'there are few more beautiful stretches of wild country in Britain than the eastern part of the Cornish highlands between the upper reaches of the Fowey and the Lynher'. Twelve Men's Moor owes its name to an agreement between the Prior and Canons of Launceston Priory and twelve tenants which was made in the thirteenth century. The boundaries of the area are set out in the document and some of the places mentioned—Boturnell, Notter Tor, the Witheybrook—can still be found on the map, as can the farms which some of the twelve men held, Castick, Browda and Trewortha. But this magic area conveys a sense of timelessness in which 600 years is as nothing.

Nowhere on the moor can you find tors more impressively sited. They all stand near the moor's edge which is adorned by the woodlands of the Trebartha estate and the lovely gorge of the Witheybrook. Closest to the edge is Hawk's Tor, not to be confused with the less impressive tor of that name in the parish of Blisland. The Hawk's Tor over Trebartha only reaches a height of 1,078ft, but it has on its eastern end a bold mass of granite fronting the Lynher valley and even rock climbers find it worth a visit. A few yards to the west of this steep crag there is a curious assembly of vertical stones which have been driven into a natural fissure in the rock. It looks as if in prehistoric times the summit of this tor was a miniature fort or stronghold. It would have been a difficult place to capture, for the hill runs steeply down on all sides but the west where this buttress has been erected. Further along the ridge is Trewortha Tor, a long straggle of rocks set in the angle made by the Witheybrook when it turns sharply from a northerly course to an easterly one. At the western end of the Trewortha ridge is the large rock basin known as King Arthur's Bed. Rock basins are frequently found on the surface of the granite. They are of varying shape and size and some of them have water standing in them all the year round. The chemical action of the standing water is one of the factors that has caused the erosion of the rock surface.

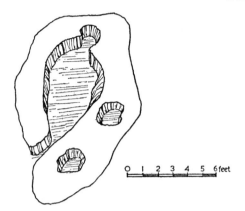

Rock basin, King Arthur's Bed, Trewortha Tor

Another is the presence of small rock particles in the depressions. These have gradually abraded the surface of the stone so that the basins are formed much in the same way as the potholes in the beds of rivers in the Yorkshire dales. King Arthur's Bed is a very large basin, rectangular in shape with a circular extension at the western end. On Fox Tor, near Altarnun, there is a circular rock basin on the side of a rock near the summit of the tor. The fact that this rock basin is in the side of the rock indicates that the boulder has fallen from its original position, for the basin must have been on the upper surface of the rock when it was incised. We see here an example of the process which causes the clitters that cover so many of the hill slopes. Rock basins excited the curiosity of the early antiquaries, particularly Borlase, who thought they were man-made objects associated with druidical worship. In his *Antiquities Historical and Monumental of the County of Cornwall* he has provided drawings of many of them.

The view of this country as you approach it over East Moor is impressive. Hawk's Tor and Trewortha Tor seem enormous and, overtopping them by another 200ft is the great arc of Kilmar with its fantastic rock castles. The half-mile summit of this hill provides an interesting and satisfying ridge walk from one cheesewring formation to the next. It is a lonely place as all these hills are. The solitary Trewartha farm-house lies in the valley below and all around is the evidence of past human endeavour—the roadways carved out for the transport of granite that was quarried here, old railway cuttings on Langstone Downs, a few ruined buildings—but all this has now been absorbed by the moor and seems an integral part of the landscape. The only alien note is struck by the afforestation above the Witheybrook on Smallacoombe Downs and some fencing on the open moor. Beyond Kilmar is a stretch of open country which includes the barrow-crowned summit of Langstone Downs and Bearah Tor, another rocky ridge like Kilmar in miniature. This wild country is easily reached from the eastern side of the moor. There is a lane which turns off the A30 at Five Lanes and takes you to the foot of Fox Tor, which could be the beginning of a splendid walk right over the eastern sector of the moor to the Cheesewring and Minions. There is a motorable road from Trebartha past Stonaford and North Bowda to Carey Tor and another from Berriow Bridge to the moor gate between Hawk's Tor and Kilmar. Bearah Tor is easily reached on foot by a rough track halfway between Kingsbeare and Henwood.

A mile to the south of Kilmar is one of the smallest but most spectacular of the Cornish tors. This is Sharp Tor, a tiny conical hill which clings to the edge of Langstone Downs, overhanging the village of Henwood. It is seen to best advantage from the road running past Notter Tor, but it is almost as arresting when viewed from the old mine workings between Minions and Henwood.

Beyond Sharp Tor is Stowe's Hill where the Cheesewring stands. On the summit is the Iron Age camp known as Stowe's Pound and on the southern side of the hill, near the Cheesewring quarry (now derelict but much used by rock climbers) stand the remains of Daniel Gumb's hut. Gumb was a stonecutter from Linkinhorne where some of his work can still be seen in the churchyard. He removed with his wife and family

Page 53 (above) King Arthur's Hall: the standing stones are what remains of the stone facing which originally surrounded the enclosure, retaining the bank; *(below)* the hut circle on Kerrow Downs remains an impressive monument. The doorway is between the prominent stones on the right. Carbilly Tor with its disused granite quarry, together with Hawk's Tor, can be seen in the distance

Page 54 (above) Barrow on Emblance Downs. The exposed cist, in deep shadow, is surrounded by standing stones; *(below)* Stowe's Pound, looking across East Cornwall to the eastern fringe of Dartmoor. The loose stone ramparts of the hill fort line the edge of the scarp

to the slopes of Stowe's Hill and inhabited a rock shelter there. This was in the first half of the eighteenth century and a Mr John Harris of Liskeard, writing 150 years later, says:

> I have a vivid recollection of visiting his Cavern with my father
> ... the entrance was rather low and narrow; the floor was full 30 feet long by 10 or 12 feet wide, composed of sandy loam inclining towards one door, opposite which was a rude chimney. On the right hand side about 3 feet high was a bench of rock running nearly the whole length from 3 to 4 feet wide, along which ran a stout fir pole. This formed the sleeping place. On the left two other benches stood, one lower than the other, serving for sitting and table. The roof was an immense slab of granite on the upper surface of which Gumb had cut some of Euclid's problems and a guttering for the purpose of collecting storm water, as well as his own name and date at the entrance which is still preserved.

This rock shelter was demolished during quarrying operations and what remains, a portion of the capstone with an incised geometrical figure and some of the rain-water channelling, lies about 100yd south-west of the original site and close to the edge of the quarry. Beside it is a stone on which is carved, 'D. Gumb, 1735'.

Daniel Gumb was a very odd character. He interested himself in mathematics and astronomy as well as the simple life. He was said to be a Deist and at his funeral at Linkinhorne in 1776, the parson in the course of his somewhat lukewarm panegyric commented, 'It is not for me to judge, suffice it to say he has not been inside the church door for the last thirty years.' Much the same might have been said about Shakespeare's Falstaff who in a moment of mock repentance observed: 'An I have not forgotten what the inside of a church is made of, I am a peppercorn, a brewer's horse: the inside of a church! Company, villanous company, hath been the spoil of me.' But there was no company, villainous or otherwise, on the slopes of Stowe's Hill in Daniel Gumb's time. The quarry had not yet been started, copper had not yet been located near the source of the Seaton river, the village of Minions had not yet been built. There was nothing for the stone-cutter to see but the raw materials of his trade, the Cheesewring towering above his head and the standing stones of the Hurlers on the lonely moor. One wonders what his long-suffering family made of it all. There is a highly coloured account of this eighteenth-century eccentric in the pages of R. S. Hawker's *Footprints of Former Men in Far Cornwall*. Beyond Stowe's Hill is Caradon, its rounded summit crowned with Bronze Age barrows. All around it are the mining villages which date from the copper boom of the nineteenth century, Minions, Upton Cross, Pensilva, Crow's Nest, Darite and Tremar. It was a busy place then as the scarred surface of the hill and the ruined engine-houses bear witness. Now it carries a television mast on its highest point with the buildings of the relay station beneath, but they hardly seem intrusive.

There is something of interest to see on every hill. On Tregarrick Tor, not far from Stowe's Hill, there is what appears to be a prehistoric rock shelter just below the highest point. A heavy slab of granite overhangs its supporting boulders and reaches out towards two small groups of upright stones placed edge to edge on the circumference of a circle. This tor stands above a shallow valley, the site of the Siblyback Reservoir and its attendant car park and club house. Tregarrick is a pleasant place to visit and so is Corner Quoit, near the moor's edge above the hamlet of Millpool in Cardinham parish. J. W. Malim calls this 'the prettiest tor on the moor'. It is an insignificant jumble of rocks and bushes piled on the 700ft contour across which a tiny stream runs to make its way past Millpool and under Cardinham church to join the Fowey. Corner Quoit is a friendly place. Colvannick, less than a mile away, only 100ft higher, another miniature rock formation, is not. It has a grandeur belied by its actual size.

South of Roughtor and Brown Willy is Garrow Tor surrounded by open moorland. From the summit you can look northward into the wild valley of the upper Delank. To the west is rolling moorland culminating in the rounded and rocky crest of Alex Tor. To the east is Butter's Tor, only 50ft lower, and all around you are the relics of the past. Garrow Tor is a solitary place now, but it has not always been so. In the Bronze Age its western slopes were occupied by a considerable number of people; in medieval times farmers came and built their long-houses on it and on the eastern slope are several houses, some of comparatively recent date, occupied within living memory. It was always the sort of place that attracted people. Car-burrow, near Warleggan, is another hill which bears much evidence of human settlement and although it lacks the charm of Garrow, it has its own individual atmosphere.

One of the factors that makes the moor so fascinating is the immense variety. Although a ridge formation is common, some of the tors like Alex Tor, Hawk's Tor in Blisland and Fox Tor, are roughly circular, standing on isolated hills while Codda Tor, Sharp Tor, Tregarrick and Carey Tor raise their rock piles on the edges of extensive hill masses which exceed them in height. Here and there are isolated piles of rock on fairly level platforms like Lanlavery Rock, north of Roughtor and Greymare Rock on East Moor. There are a number of perched rocks, such as you would expect to find in a glaciated region,

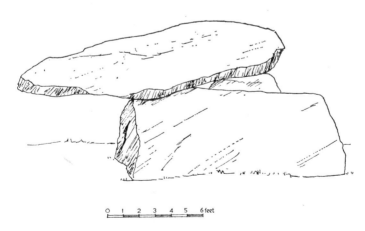

Perched rock, Bedrawle – possibly a prehistoric rock shelter

standing on hillsides. A prominent example is the Elephant Rock half-way down the southern slope of Hendra Beacon and there is another much smaller one at Bradford, near the bottom of the first enclosed field north of the river. These will have been left in their present positions by the movement of the melted sludge carried down the hillsides in the ice age. The enormous boulder on the south-eastern bank of the Delank river, just above Bedrawle Bridge, probably owes its present location to the same cause. Not far away the bed of the stream is covered with giant boulders through which, in times of drought, the Delank river makes its way by a series of tiny rivulets. Bodmin Moor is an intensely interesting region for the geomorphologist, but its physical features and wide varieties of scene are also a delight to the visitor who has no specialised knowledge.

3   ANCIENT TIMES

IF you walk across the moor in summer or early autumn you may be quite unaware of the relics of the past which lie around you, but if you come again when winter has transformed the moor into a dun waste, relieved only by the deep green of the broom and furze bushes and the grey of the granite, you will discover that you are surrounded by a wealth of evidence of early occupation. Few areas in this country have so many traces of early man. Within the limits of the Camel, the Inney, the Lynher and the Fowey the one-inch or new metric map records close on 100 tumuli and nearly 30 hut settlements but even this total may be an underestimate. The granite regions of the South West were very attractive to prehistoric man. These upland areas were both well watered and more or less free from the luxuriant growth which made settlement in the lower valleys so difficult. The climate, too, was more favourable for human settlement than it is today—the uplands were warmer and drier.

Many memorials of the past although damaged, have survived. The durability of the stone of which they are made and the remoteness of the areas in which they are found have ensured their preservation. The moor is full of interest to the archaeologist and it is a part of its paradoxical nature that though it is an area of lonely remoteness, it is a palimpsest on which man has made his mark since very early times. You cannot move far without seeing an ancient field hedge or hut circle, a stone ring or a ruined camp. The shallow river valleys are full of grass-grown spoil heaps left by the old tin streamers and the moorland is criss-crossed by the leats they made.

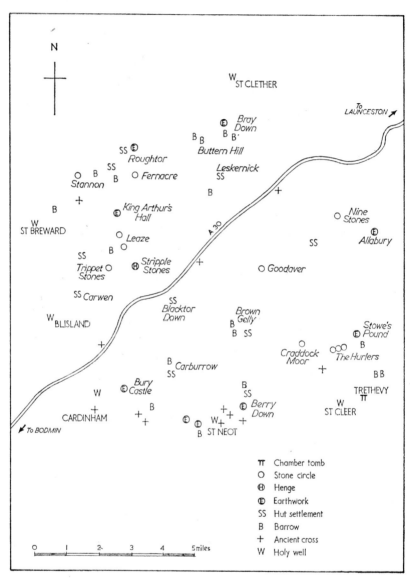

N

W ST CLETHER

To LAUNCESTON ↗

Ⓔ Bray Down
B B·

B B

Buttern Hill

SS Ⓔ Roughtor

Leskernick
SS

SS

B Stannon B

O Fernacre

B

+

O Nine Stones

B

Ⓔ King Arthur's Hall

Ⓔ Allabury

W ST BREWARD

A 30

SS

O Leaze

+

W ST BREWARD

SS

B O

Ⓗ Stripple Stones

+

O Goodaver

Trippet Stones

SS Carwen

SS Blacktor Down

Brown Gelly
B

Stowe's Ⓔ Pound

W BLISLAND

+

B SS

B OOO The Hurlers

O Craddock Moor

B

B Carburrow
SS

B SS

+

BB

W CARDINHAM

Ⓔ Bury Castle

B

+

B SS

Ⓔ Berry Down

TRETHEVY
ͲͲ

+

+

+

W +

W ST CLEER

↙ To BODMIN

Ⓔ Ⓔ W+ +

B ST NEOT

ͲͲ	Chamber tomb
O	Stone circle
Ⓗ	Henge
Ⓔ	Earthwork
SS	Hut settlement
B	Barrow
+	Ancient cross
W	Holy well

0 1 2 3 4 5 miles

Principal antiquities

In certain areas there is so much evidence of the past that one can hardly walk twenty paces without coming across some object of archaeological interest. A good example is Carburrow Tor in the parish of Warleggan. Its summit is crowned with Bronze Age barrows; nearby is a chamber tomb of earlier date and the south-eastern hillside is covered with a cluster of hut circles. At Tor Farm, just outside the moor hedge and within 20yd of the present house and farm buildings, stand the remains of a medieval long-house which was itself erected within a few yards of a Bronze Age dwelling. Tor has been settled for close on 4,000 years. Only a couple of hundred yards away is Whitewalls, where a farm building just across the yard from the Victorian farmhouse incorporates three of the outside walls of its Elizabethan predecessor. The long-house which preceded that no longer exists, but its outlines could be traced fifty years ago, and 20yd higher up the hill the scatter of hut circles remain. On Carburrow the sense of continuity is strong.

So it is on Garrow Tor, where relics of the Bronze and Iron Age and medieval times stand in close proximity, and on the slopes of Roughtor where stone circles, barrows, hut settlements and an Iron Age camp are dangerously near the china-clay workings of the present century.

No traces of Paleolithic man have been discovered on Bodmin Moor but the Middle Stone Age is well represented on the moor by a number of microliths (small flint implements) found on the shores of Dozmary Pool, which seems to have been a centre for the manufacture of these tools. There is no indigenous flint nearer to Cornwall than Beer Head on the eastern borders of Devon, but flint pebbles are sometimes washed up on the Cornish coast. They may have been found in sufficient quantities to provide raw material for the manufacture of the Mesolithic implements found at Dozmary Pool and also in the Land's End district and the Lizard peninsula. The implements are small, about 1in long with sharp edge and point.

Flint flakes, a few arrowheads and some greenstone axes of the Neolithic period are sometimes picked up on the moor and during World War II, when a good deal of land went under the plough, a number of flint implements were found in fields to the west of Bolventor. Neolithic man has left one elaborate, though severely mutilated, monument on the moor. This is the Stripple Stones, one of the three henges known to exist in Cornwall. It was excavated in 1907 but no finds emerged. Similarly, the henge at Castilly, close to the A30 trunk road some seven miles south of the moor, yielded no datable material when it was investigated in 1962. Possibly the Cornish henges are contemporary with the famous henge at Arminghall, Norfolk, which was constructed at some time during the period 2400–2100 BC.

The Stripple Stones stand on the shoulder of Hawk's Tor in the parish of Blisland about half-way between the summit and the Hawk's Tor clayworks. The monument consists of a care-

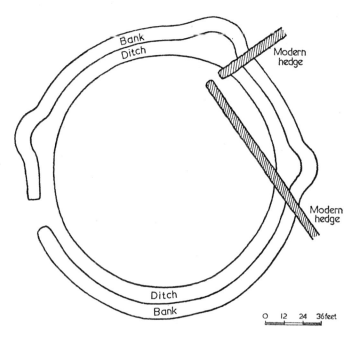

The Stripple Stones, Neolithic henge

fully levelled circular platform surrounded by a ditch with a raised bank beyond it. Clearly it is not a fortification because the ditch is inside the bank which expands at three points into curved extensions or demilunes. The central platform, about 145ft in diameter, was originally occupied by a circle of twenty-eight standing stones and a massive central monolith. Only four of the stones now stand and though there are a few fallen stones on the platform most of them have disappeared. In the late 1880s two field hedges were built into the monument. Some of the standing stones were used in their construction and a segment of the circle was obliterated.

The relics of the past on Bodmin Moor are impressive because of their number rather than their individual quality. 'But it hath bene a large thinge', said John Leland of Tintagel Castle, but he would have found nothing on the moor to provoke such a comment. Bodmin Moor has no Avebury, no Stonehenge, no Maiden Castle. But close to the old mining village of Darite in the parish of St Cleer is a chamber-tomb known as Trethevy Quoit, which is unquestionably the finest of the megalithic tombs for which Cornwall is famous. It was a sea-borne people from south-west Europe who brought this cult to our island and the Cornish examples are chiefly found in the Isles of Scilly and West Penwith. Indeed, there are only three specimens in central Cornwall, at Pawton near Wadebridge, at Lesquite near Lanivet and Trethevy which is the most impressive of them all. You come on it unexpectedly by driving or walking up the sunken lane from Darite and there it is, standing grandly in the field above, with its great capstone covering a burial chamber that is nearly 9ft high. It still looks exactly as it did when Norden described it nearly 400 years ago, 'a little howse raysed of mightie stones standing on a little hill within a fielde'. The little hill is all that remains of the long barrow which at one time covered it, for natural erosion and the depredations of medieval farmers have robbed it of the earth and stones of which it was composed. The burial chamber itself remains as it was when it was constructed 3,500 years ago, except for the

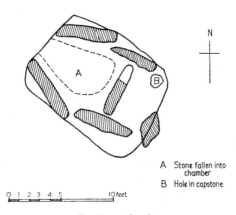

A   Stone fallen into chamber

B   Hole in capstone

Trethevy Quoit

fact that one stone slab has fallen inwards into the chamber.
Six large blocks of moorstone enclose an area measuring
7ft × 5ft × 8ft 8in high. The capstone which covers the
chamber has a hole in one corner. Whether the hole was
chipped out by the megalith builders, or whether it was caused
by natural erosion, its presence would obviously have facilitated
the manoeuvering of this enormously heavy block of granite into
position. At the south-eastern end of the monument is a recess
or antechamber constructed by overlapping the end stone with
the two most easterly of the side slabs. The granite block that
has been overlapped and that closes the chamber on this side,
has had one corner cut out of it, leaving an aperture through
which it is possible to crawl. Glyn Daniel in the *Prehistoric
Chamber Tombs of England and Wales* (1950) says that Trethevy is
a single collective tomb used for burial only once, but when the
chamber tomb at West Lanyon, near Land's End, was opened
in 1800, human bones were found 'lying in a promiscuous state
and a disordered manner', which suggests a disarray caused by
successive burials. Trethevy may have been used in this way,
but as the barrow that covered it had been removed long before
Norden's time and the contents of the tomb dispersed we shall
never know.

Trethevy is the only accepted chamber tomb in the Bodmin Moor area, but there is a related structure on the north-west slope of Carburrow Tor. From the larger of the two cairns on the summit an ancient hedge, the stones of which are now spread over the ground, leads straight downhill in a north-westerly direction for about 50yd and ends at the point where a great block of granite covers a rock-lined chamber measuring about 5ft × 4ft × 3ft. There is good access to this cavity from the south and more limited access from the east, where two shallow and rough-hewn steps lead down to it. The capstone, a large, rectangular granite block, approximately 12ft × 6ft × 3ft, is supported on smaller pieces of rock and lies in a horizontal position although the ground slopes quite steeply. It is hard to believe that it occupies its present position by chance.

Another even more debatable collection of rocks can be found on Treswallock Downs about 100yd due north of the point where the lane from Treswallock Farm turns sharply to the right on its way to St Breward village. Its position, rather low down on the hillside, is an unlikely site for a megalithic monument, although the arrangement of the granite slabs suggests a chamber tomb. The moor offers considerable scope for prehistoric 'discoveries' of this kind. The difference between a man-made megalithic structure and a natural rock formation is sometimes slight and it is easy to be deceived. Nevertheless, it is doubtful if all the evidence of early occupation of this area has been recorded. Archaeological investigation of Bodmin Moor has been intermittent and scanty and much remains to be located and examined.

Most familiar of all the ancient monuments are the stone circles of which there are no less than eleven on Bodmin Moor. They are roughly contemporary with the Trethevy tomb and date from about 1500 BC. Best known and most easily reached are the Hurlers, near Minions, a complex of three circles standing close together 200yd north of the village. They owe their name to the legend that they were men turned into stone for profaning the Lord's Day by playing the Cornish game of hurling, the game that is still played at St Columb every Shrove Tuesday. The changing of men into stone is a recurrent theme in Norse mythology, but the Sabbath breaking variant of it seems to be a Puritan story. Norden, writing in 1584, knew the name but does not mention the legend. Twenty years later Carew refers to the 'country people's report that once they were men and for their hurling upon the Sabbath, so metamorphosed'. Nearby are two massive stones standing close together. They are more regular in shape than the stones of the circles themselves and it is not known if they are associated with them. An investigation carried out at the Hurlers reveals that part of the area within the most northerly circle was roughly paved and a pavement 6ft wide had been constructed between that circle and the central one.

The circles on Bodmin Moor vary in size. The three that make up the Hurlers, the Trippet Stones, Goodaver and Craddock Moor Circles have diameters that vary from 104 to 135ft. The two Leaze circles and the Nine Stones circle on East Moor are smaller, like those in West Penwith. The Nine Stones circle was restored by the squire of Trebartha in 1889 when all but two of the stones had fallen. There are now eight standing stones around the circumference and one in the centre, but the central stone is almost certainly later in date than the others and forms part of an alignment that marks the parish boundary of Altarnun and North Hill. Goodaver, on the hilltop above the Fowey, has been restored, too. This was done at the beginning of this century by a local parson. Unfortunately, some of the stones have been re-erected upside down and some were not restored to their original sockets. But Goodaver is the most dramatically sited of all the Bodmin Moor circles. You can see it cutting the skyline two miles away from the high ground above Dozmary.

On the western side of the moor are the stone circles of Stannon and Fernacre which are different from the others. The stones are more numerous—at Stannon over seventy remain—they are smaller and more irregularly spaced. These monuments are larger than any of the other Cornish stone circles and the builders did not take the precaution of mapping out the circumference with a thong so neither circle is perfect. The reason for these differences is not known. It has been suggested that they are later than the others and that they are degenerate examples of a tradition imperfectly understood, but there is no evidence to support this. The stone circles generate some very fanciful thinking. For instance, there is the theory of A. L. Lewis who published a paper on the Bodmin Moor circles in 1898. After taking a number of measurements of the diameters of the circles and of the distances between some of them, worked out on the six inch map, he satisfied himself that the measurements were divisible in whole numbers by a distance of 25.1in, the length of the Egyptian or Royal Persian cubit and went on to say:

> It may therefore not be unreasonable to suppose that someone from some country bordering on the Mediterranean may have visited Cornwall as a merchant, explorer or refugee, or possibly as a slave carried there for sale, and that being there he was employed by the local chief in the construction of his public works and made use of a measure which he happened to have with him.

Stone circles inspire a good many fantastic notions for the lack of real evidence provides room for any amount of theorising, but despite many ingenious suggestions we still have no real idea of their original function. They simply exist. And as you walk in the rain across East Moor towards the Nine Stones Circle, or Manor Common towards the Trippet Stones, you can be forgiven for thinking of the fallen Titans in *Hyperion*:

> . . . like a dismal cirque
> Of Druid Stones upon a forlorn moor
> When the chill rain begins at shut of eve
> In dull November . . .

These simple but powerful relics of the past will turn anyone into a romantic.

In addition to the stone circles and roughly contemporary with them, are the barrows. On the moorland area the Ordnance Survey map indicates 'Tumulus' or 'Tumuli' no less than 41 times. Even without detailed investigation it is obvious that barrows are of many different kinds. Some, like those on Carburrow or Brown Gelly are large cairns of loose stone, some are turf-covered mounds with or without a deep depression in the summit, some are only recognisable when you come close to them and all that can be seen is a small circle, or part of a circle, of standing stones placed edge to edge, enclosing a stone box or cist which is open to the sky. Some of the barrows have been denuded as the result of natural erosion and some have been stripped by grave robbers, the early antiquaries and also treasure-hunters whose activities have been extensive. A prominent barrow on the hill between the Hurlers and the Cheesewring reveals in its side a stone cist where a secondary burial was made. Early in the last century a group of miners who were removing earth from the barrow came across it and rifled it. One of the objects found was a corrugated gold cup, 3½in high. It seems to be of Greek workmanship and is similar to a pair of cups found in one of the royal tombs in Mycenae. This cup came into royal hands too; King William IV acquired it and, if the story is true, used it as a shaving mug. It is now in the British Museum and a replica can be seen at the County Museum, Truro.

Not only do barrows vary a great deal in external appearance, they seem to have been constructed for different purposes. Barrows are usually thought of as graves, mounds thrown up to cover an inhumation or cremation but this is not invariably the case. Some of the barrows investigated by Borlase, though undisturbed before he dug them, revealed no human burials and recent investigation of some barrows in the china-clay area near St Austell, has demonstrated that some of these structures were built over elaborate ritual areas in which human burial played no part. There is a note in *Cornish Archaeology*, no 11 of an investigation at Caerloggas, near St Austell. This records a ritual enclosure of most elaborate construction. An area surrounded by a slight ditch was approached by a causeway to an entrance defined by two standing stones. The enclosed area had been levelled and surrounded by a double ring of posts, subsequently removed, and a layer of yellow clay brought from some distance had been applied. A ritual pit contained some scraps of burnt bone, flints and white pebbles. More flints and pebbles and an Early Bronze Age dagger were found in the enclosure. There were two barrows adjacent to the enclosure, one largely destroyed, but the other was undamaged. The yellow clay had been used again here. The undamaged barrow contained no burial.

In 1955 a barrow at Tregulland on Wilsey Down which is a northern extension of Bodmin Moor was totally excavated. The first burial, an inhumation, had been disturbed but the rest of the barrow was untouched. The primary burial had been surrounded by two circles of stakes subsequently removed and replaced by a cairn ring faced by a wall, which had built into it some cup-marked slabs of slate. Ritual fires had been lit in a pit outside the central area. There was also a cremation burial with arrowheads associated with it and another cremation with food vessels.

Tregulland and Caerloggas have some features in common and it is clear that Bronze Age barrows are something more than burial places; they are evidence of an elaborate cult of religious significance. Barrows with central pits dug into the top may have been built in that way and the pits are not invariably the result of later disturbance. It is clear, too, that many of the barrows as we now see them are the result of a series of constructive processes carried out over a long period of time.

On Bodmin Moor the numerous 'denuded' barrows which lie on hillsides or comparatively low ground were not necessarily covered by large mounds or cairns. There are a number of these on the open moor between Stannon and Fernacre circles; there is an excellent example on Emblance Downs about 300yd

north-west of Leaze farm gate and there is another just outside
the moor gate, near the track which runs northwards from
Bradford in the direction of Bolatherick. There is no evidence
in any of these places of stones or soil which may have originally
covered these barrows and some of them are so remotely
situated that it is unlikely that any top covering has been
carried away. It is a reasonable assumption that these structures never looked very different from how they appear today.

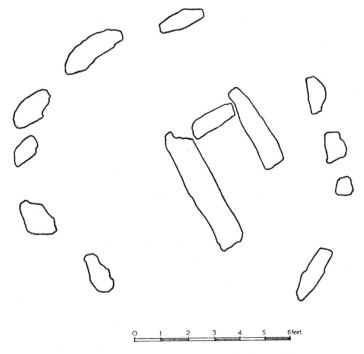

Denuded barrow and exposed cist on Emblance Downs

The most common of all archaeological remains on the moor
are the hut settlements. As we see them now, these consist of
circles of upright stones of varying diameters. They are generally linked with field walls which enclose small irregular
fields. The hut circles are mostly found on the southern or

Page 71 (left) Cross on Craddock Moor; this impressive monument stands on a wide expanse of open moor near the Redgate–Minions road; Tregarrick Tor is in the distance; *(right)* St Neot cross-shaft; this is tenth-century work, if not a little earlier; it is the finest ornamented cross-shaft in Cornwall

Page 72 (above) Circular hut in Leaze farmyard; formerly a piggery or toolshed, its date is unknown; (below) Delphy Bridge; this primitive-looking clapper bridge is less than 100 years old and carries the moorland road from Blisland to St Breward across the Delank

south-eastern slopes of the hills with their doorways, usually easily recognisable, facing away from the prevailing wind. Sometimes they have the added protection of a porch or flanking wall. The tradition of building these circular huts persisted for many centuries and only excavation and the discovery of datable finds will determine their approximate age. The bulk of them belong to the Bronze Age when Bodmin Moor must have carried a much larger population than it does today. As we have seen, the climate in the second millennium BC was much better than it has been in recent times. Some collections of huts indicate a sizeable village. There are more than fifty of them on the slopes of Leskernick Hill in the upper Fowey valley; there is an even larger village on Blacktor Downs near Temple, where the huts cluster thickly on the hillside almost down to the stream. There are also large settlements on the lower slopes of Roughtor and on the eastern side of Brown Gelly.

Small settlements, each consisting of half a dozen huts or so, are numerous. There is an excellent example on Kerrow Downs about 100yd to the north-west of the road from Bradford to Blisland and another, nearer Blisland village, at Carwen where the huts are constructed of massive blocks of moorstone. Single huts are rarer for the builders of these settlements seem to have been a gregarious people.

In volume 9 of *Cornish Archaeology* is published the report of a detailed examination of a group of huts on Stannon Down, near Roughtor. This was a rescue operation undertaken in 1968 when these huts were under threat of being submerged beneath the overburden tip of the Stannon clayworks. Eighteen huts were surveyed and eight of them totally excavated. The huts, with internal diameters that varied from 33ft to 19ft, had thick walls which were originally about 3½ft high. These must have supported rafters which ran to a central post and in all the huts there was evidence of a ring of secondary supports 8 or 9ft from the centre. The entrance passages and some parts of the interiors of the huts were paved, and paving slabs also covered the drains and sumps which had been constructed in some of the huts. Small post holes were discovered and these probably indicate the provision of internal furnishings, beds, cupboards and partitions. In one of the huts there were carefully constructed alcoves set in the walls, probably for storage purposes. Gulleys had been dug around the outside of the walls of some of the huts to drain away rainwater from the roof.

The acid soil of Bodmin Moor is unkind to pottery, but a number of sherds were found along with about fifty fragments of flint, mostly chippings or flakes. Two greenstone artefacts were discovered, an axe about 6in long and an 'adze' or hoe. Most of the pottery is similar to material found at Gwithian in west Cornwall which is dated somewhere between 2000 and 1500 BC. It seems likely that there were two phases of occupation of the site, the first in the period 2000–1500 BC and the second about 1150 BC. The settlement was probably abandoned some 250 years later, perhaps because of the deterioration of the climate.

The investigators found it impossible to draw firm conclusions about the adjoining field system. Many ancient fields were already covered by the china-clay spoil heaps and there are other hut circles in the vicinity, so that it is impossible to decide how far the fields of this particular community stretched. Some of the fields are fairly large and it is thought that these were used to pasture stock. It was noted that the walls enclosing these fields were carefully constructed of small rubble held together with large flat stones placed transversely, which suggests that they were built to enclose animals and were not merely the result of the clearance of surface stone from the land. Others consist of narrow strips running with the slope of the land. These were probably arable fields, ploughed up and down, The rough walls bordering them are the result of field clearance. The discovery of three saddle querns in one of the huts indicates that cereals were grown, but it is estimated that only $1\frac{3}{4}$ acres of land in close proximity to the settlement were under corn, so that amounts must have been very small. It seems that the downs were chiefly used, as they still are, for grazing stock, though some land was dug or ploughed. We know that spades were used at Stannon, for the drains in one of the huts reveal spade marks. We know, too, from an examination of the ancient field systems in various parts of the moor that some of the land was under cultivation. Some of the fields reveal lynchets, terraces formed by the worked soil as it crept downhill on steep slopes. Lynchets can be clearly seen on Langstone Downs facing the marshes near the source of the Witheybrook. They are in close proximity to a large group of hut circles.

Though the Stannon huts date from the Bronze Age it must not be assumed that all hut circles belong to this period. Close to a farm-house on the eastern side of Garrow Tor is a small circular hut, its walls similar in construction to those built in Bronze Age times. This was used up to the present century as a tool shed or pigsty and may have been built quite recently. There is a similar hut in the yard of Leaze farm-house.

The Iron Age was a period of immigration from the continent. There were three main incursions. The first, known to archaeology as Iron Age A, occurred in the fifth and fourth centuries BC, and is recognised by its pottery and weapons. It does not seem to have made much impact in the south-western peninsula. The second, Iron Age B, dates from the third and second centuries BC, and the last, as the result of the invasion of Gaul by Germanic tribes, reached Britain at the end of the second century BC and continued for some fifty years. It was the second of these three incursions which mainly affected Cornwall. These Celtic invaders are our ancestors and brought with them the language that was to become Cornish. They seem to have been a vigorous and bellicose people, fitting forerunners of the Cornishmen who marched to Blackheath in 1497, or those who, fifty years later, played their part in the Prayer Book Rebellion. Their chief impact on Bodmin Moor is revealed in the considerable number of hill camps and fortified enclosures which stand around the moor's edge.

Only detailed examination of a number of hut settlements on the moor would reveal if these were occupied by Celtic people.

75

It seems likely that the deterioration of climate that set in at the beginning of the last millennium before Christ was the cause of a steady depopulation of the moorland area. We have seen that the Bronze Age settlement on Stannon Down was abandoned at approximately 900 BC, a time when these granite uplands were becoming unattractive to the farmer. Detailed examination of other hut settlements on the moor might reveal that they also were vacated at about the same period, for people tend to imitate each other. Iron Age man was better equipped to clear the forests in the valleys than his Bronze Age predecessors and such areas would be much more attractive to him.

There are, however, two references on Bodmin Moor to a feature characteristic of the late Iron Age—the fogou. The name is derived from the Cornish 'fogo' which means a cave and it is an underground chamber or passage always found in association with human settlements. There is a fine example at Carn Euny, near Sancreed and there are several others in the west of Cornwall. It was believed at one time that these structures were designed as hiding places, but it is much more likely that they were communal cellars for the preservation of food. There are records of a fogou at West Carne in the parish of Altarnun. In 1887 it was reported that when a field known as the Church Close was ploughed, the share sometimes grated on granite slabs which were the covering stones of an underground passage. Hencken, writing in 1932, states that the fogou has been destroyed and Evelyn Clark, the author of *Cornish Fogous* says that when she examined the site in 1954 she could find no evidence of it apart from a few low mounds. The fogou marked on the one-inch map on the northern slopes of Maiden Tor, near Brown Willy, does not exist either and it is hard to believe that such a bleak and exposed spot could be the site of a hut settlement.

The fortified enclosures which stand around the edge of the moor do not necessarily indicate Iron Age occupation of the moor itself. It is unlikely that they were permanently occupied, but were used in an emergency by those living on lower ground. The last three centuries before Christ were an uneasy time with numerous incursions into Cornwall from Europe and those who came had to protect themselves from later arrivals. The camps, or rounds, most of them quite small, are sited on the hilltops or higher slopes around the edge of the moor, mostly in the south. But on the west, Roughtor, which stands only a couple of miles from the Camel valley and which is almost a fortress in itself, shows remains of a hill fort at its north-western end. The boulders that formed the drystone rampart are plainly visible between Little Roughtor and the summit of its taller neighbour. At the northern end of the moor, on the lower slopes of Bray Down, there is a single-banked enclosure a couple of hundred yards above the lane which runs along the edge of the moor between West Carne and Bowithick. Not far away is another round, or earthwork, on the banks of the Penpont Water.

On the east is the earthwork known as Allabury. This stands half-way down the slope that rises to Hawk's Tor beside the tumbling Witheybrook. Further to the south is the dramatic hilltop fortress of Stowe's Pound. Both parts of its present name are Saxon but the defences were erected by Iron Age Celts. Like Trencrom, a contour fort on a granite hill near St Ives, Stowe's Pound has drystone walls which make skilful use of the natural bastions of rock lining the summit of the Cheesewring hill. It would have been a difficult place to attack, for on all sides except the north, where there is a second line of defence, the slopes are precipitous. Stowe's Pound is intensely evocative of the past; there are few places in this haunting country that are more so.

Six miles further to the west on Berry Down in St Neot is an earthwork of a different kind. It lies a little below the highest point of the hill and incorporates a natural ridge of rock on its southern side. The enclosed area leans towards the south, protecting itself not only from its human and animal enemies, but also from the north-west winds which whip across the moor. Within it are a number of hut circles and there are traces of outer fortifications to the east and north. The place has none of the stark atmosphere of Stowe's Pound and it was probably a fortified farmstead rather than a hill fort. Across the valley of the Loveny is another earthwork which lies below the highest point of the hill. This is the so-called 'Roman camp', an Iron Age fortified enclosure now largely ploughed out, though still plainly visible. Bury Castle, above Cardinham, is also situated below the highest point of the ridge on which it stands, but this is a more important fortification than the earthworks in St Neot. It is larger and its ramparts are higher. To the east and south-east the land falls steeply to a small stream. On this side the enclosure is guarded by a single bank and ditch. On the west where the land slopes gently upwards, the fort is guarded by additional ramps and ditches of which only scanty traces remain.

Mention should be made of three earthworks, rectangular in shape which, so far, have defined analysis. One of these is the Crowpound on Goonzion Downs in St Neot. This measures approximately 160ft by 120ft. The walls are clearly defined, but the centre of the enclosure has been seriously disturbed by open-cast mining operations. This monument has found a place in the extensive hagiography of the patron saint of the parish, for we are told that St Neot impounded the crows here during the hours of divine worship so that the farmers had no excuse for neglecting their religious obligations. This legend must have become a part of the folk-consciousness after East Cornwall had abandoned the native speech and had forgotten that 'crows' is Cornish for cross. The cross which gave the earthwork its name now stands in the churchyard. The date of the Crowpound is unknown. Its rectangular shape has given rise to the supposition that it was built by the Romans, though there are no other Roman remains in the vicinity. It is just as likely to be a medieval cattle pound or it may even date from the Bronze Age.

There is another rectangular enclosure on the south-eastern slopes of Carburrow just behind Whitewalls farm. It has a sloping surface but the rake is not so pronounced as that of the hillside into which it is built. It is obvious, therefore, that it has been dug out. Its walls have the appearance of being roughly contemporary with those of the numerous Bronze Age huts which stand close by.

The third rectangular building is a more impressive monument. It stands high on open moor alongside an ancient trackway between Middle Candra and Garrow Tor. The interior of the enclosure has been scooped out, leaving a walled-in area measuring internally 158ft by 65ft. The walls were retained by large granite slabs, a number of which remain, although they have suffered a good deal from the depredations of cattle. The monument has recently been fenced in to save it from further damage. Norden describes it as 'a square plott . . . situate on a playne Mountayne, wrowghte some 3 foote into the grounde, and by reason of the depression of the place, ther standeth a stange or Poole of water, the place sett rounde aboute with flatt stones'. His description will serve equally well today. This curious structure is too large to have carried a roof and it has been suggested that it was a medieval cattle pound, as perhaps the Crowpound was, or even a reservoir, though there seems to be no good reason why either should be sited on this 'playne Mountayne', exposed to every wind that blows and within easy reach of running water.

Norden knew this enclosure as King Arthur's Hall, 'a place so called and by tradition helde to be a place wherunto that famous K. Arthur resorted', and it still bears the name today. It is not the only place in this small area that is associated with Arthur. Dozmary Pool is held to be the lake to which Sir Bedivere consigned Arthur's sword, Excalibur, after 'that last weird battle in the west'; Trethevy Quoit is sometimes known as Arthur's Quoit and the large rock basin at the western end of Trewortha Tor is called King Arthur's Bed. Borlase, the eighteenth-century antiquary, seems to have known this particular feature. 'Some of these Basons,' he writes, 'have one part of their hollow made more circular than the rest as if it were to reserve the head, and the other part of the body of some human

79

creature', and he writes of the supposed druidical practice of treating patients 'for particular disorders' by laying them in the rock basin, 'that by the healing virtue attributed to the god who inhabited the Rock they might be cured of their ailment'. If Borlase knew that the man-shaped rock basin on Trewortha Tor was associated with Arthur he does not say so, but he comments elsewhere that 'whatever is great and the use and Author unknown, is in Cornwall, for the most part attributed to King Arthur'.

The name of Arthur is writ large over the whole of this part of the county. Castle Killibury, or Kelly Rounds, the earthwork above Egloshayle, is said to be the ancient Kelliwic of Arthurian legend and Tregear Rounds between St Endellion and Delabole is one of the places identified with the Castle of Damelioc. Camelford, not very confidently, has been regarded as Arthur's Camelot. The barrow within the walls of the Iron Age camp on Warbstow Bury, a few miles to the north of Bodmin Moor, is known as Arthur's Grave and so is Condolden Barrow to the north of Camelford. There is also the inscribed stone which lies beside the Camel little more than a mile to the south-east of Condolden at Slaughter Bridge. This was one of the supposed sites of Camlann, 'the last dismal battle strooken between the noble King Arthur and his treacherous nephew Mordred, wherein the one took his death and the other his death's wound. For testimony whereof the old folk thereabouts still show you a stone bearing Arthur's name though now depraved to Atry'. Carew is wide of the mark for the inscription on the stone, still plainly visible, runs, *Latini ic jacit filius Magari*—(the monument of) Latinus. Here he lies, son of Magarus'. Wishful thinking could identify the letters *agari* at the end of the inscription as *Atry*, for the *g* and *a* can be read as *tr* and the *r* and *i* are run together and look very like *y*. This valley near the source of the Camel is the site of a battle and Leland mentions that 'people fynd there yn plowing Bones and Harneys', but the battle that yielded these remains was fought during the Saxon invasion of Cornwall. This was in AD 825, 300 years after Camlann.

This wealth of Arthurian topographical reference owes much to the wide currency of Geoffrey of Monmouth's fictional identification of Tintagel as Arthur's birthplace. The 'Arthurian' castle which superseded the building erected just after the Conquest was built shortly after Reginald, an illegitimate son of Henry I, was created Earl of Cornwall in 1141. Earl Robert of Gloucester, his half-brother, was a patron of Geoffrey of Monmouth and this, together with the romantic and impressive site of the new castle on its remote headland, may have caused Geoffrey to choose Tintagel as the scene of his hero's birth. As E. K. Chambers has written, 'No work of imagination, save the *Aeneid*, has done more to shape the legend of a people than the *Historia Regum Britanniae* of a writer who describes himself in his prefatory epistles as Gaufridus Monemutensis.'

But Arthur was well established in the local folk-consciousness before Geoffrey's *History of Britain* appeared. In 1113, over twenty years before it was written, some canons of Laon visited England with miracle-working relics to raise money for the rebuilding of their cathedral. As they made their way through Devon they were told that they were in King Arthur's own country and were shown Arthur's Chair and Arthur's Oven. When they came to Bodmin a quarrel arose between one of them and a Cornishman with a withered arm who had come to them to be healed. The foreigners and local men soon came to blows, the point at issue being that the men of Laon said that Arthur was dead and the Bodmin men insisted that he was still alive. Here is the 'rex quondam et rex futurus' theme firmly established in mid-Cornwall before Geoffrey of Monmouth published the story that has so greatly benefited the tourist trade.

Some forty years ago Collingwood wrote:

> ... the historicity (of Arthur) can hardly be called in question. The fact that his name in later ages was a magnet drawing to itself all manner of folk-lore and fable and that an Arthurian cycle grew up composed partly of events transferred from other contexts, no more proves him a fictitious character than similar

fables prove it of Alexander or Aristotle, Vergil or Roland. It tends rather to prove the opposite. The place which the name of Arthur occupies in Celtic legend is easier to explain on the hypothesis that he really lived and was a great champion of the British people.

Since Collingwood's *Roman Britain* was written, belief in his assertion has strengthened. The work of Ralegh Radford, Alcock and others has illuminated the Dark Ages and the existence of Arthur as an historical character is assured. In *Arthur's Britain*, published in 1971, Leslie Alcock writes, 'He was not a King, and unlike the warlords of the Germanic and Celtic heroic societies, he founded no dynasty. He was instead the leader of the combined forces of the small kingdoms into which sub-Roman Britain had dissolved.' The locality of the battles in which he was victorious, as cited by Nennius, is uncertain but may have ranged as far afield as Somerset, Chester, Lincolnshire and Scotland. None of them is likely to have taken place in Cornwall.

But the Cornish took him to themselves. Carew, with Geoffrey of Monmouth and Malory in mind, could write with assurance, 'In descending to martial men Arthur claimeth the first mention, a Cornishman by birth, a King of Britain by succession', and it was natural, indeed it was inevitable, that among the many places in this island where the local topography rings with 'the matter of Britain', Celtic Cornwall should be numbered. So Arthur is commemorated in a number of places that stir the imagination. The Iron Age hill forts from Tregear Rounds to Castle-an-Dinas, the great Bronze Age barrows that mark the last resting place of some unknown chieftain gain added lustre from his name. Dozmary Pool's associations with Arthur are probably quite recent and owe more to Tennyson and Robert Stephen Hawker than they do to ancient legend or historical fact. It is interesting to note that Michell in his *Parochial History of St Neots* (1833) refers to the Tregeagle legend when describing Dozmary, but makes no mention of Arthur, for he was writing before Tennyson had given the Arthurian legend a fresh wave of popularity. But by the end of the nineteenth century no topographical work could afford to mention Dozmary Pool without bringing Arthur, Excalibur and the Lady of the Lake into the account.

Here on these rolling uplands we are surrounded by relics of the past. A few of them have been scientifically investigated and evaluated but much remains to be done. What has been clear down through the ages is that the ancient tombs and ritual areas, the stone circles, the hill forts and the remains of early human settlement have captured the imagination of all those who have seen them. So the legends have grown. Men have been turned into stones, Arthur has built his hall on an empty hilltop or lain in his stone bed, the Druids have practised their rites. The old stories must have seemed far-fetched even to those who propagated them, but it was a way of expressing their awareness of the sense of the numinous that these ancient monuments generate. As time goes on, much that is at present a matter for speculation will be resolved. In the meantime, Bodmin Moor remains a richly endowed archaeological area, awaiting further detailed investigation to widen our knowledge of the distant past.

4   THE MORE RECENT PAST

AFTER the depopulation of the moor which took place during the last millennium before Christ, the area seems to have been sparsely occupied up to the time of the Norman Conquest. The Domesday manors of Fawton, Rillaton, Hamatethy and Henliston stretched far into the moor but their considerable moorland areas were wastes used only for summer pasturage. We find that most of the place names in the centre of the moor are Saxon in origin, not Celtic. Roughland, Dairywell, Fernacre, Bradford, Blacktor, Hardhead, Shallow Water, Rushyford and Witheybrook are Saxon names and might be found anywhere in England. On the edge of the moor, however, we find names typically Cornish like Menaglaze, Penkestle, Treveddoe, Treswigger, Carbaglet, Trevague and Trewint. The most prominent hills which can be seen from a distance generally have Cornish, or corrupted Cornish names like Brown Gelly, Brown Willy, Kilmar, Caradon and Hendra and the only hill in this category with an English name is Roughtor, perhaps because it is so accessible. The smaller hills, Fox Tor, Sharp Tor, Hawk's Tor, Hill Tor, Berry Down and Tolborough seem to have acquired their names after the English occupied the area. The settlement of the moor was a Saxon affair.

By AD 1200 the population of Cornwall was three times what it was at the time of the Norman Conquest and there was some land hunger, so the moor was resettled. The Knights Templar built a hospice in the centre of the moor at a place still called Temple, and some of the moor farms that are still occupied were established then. The Canons of Launceston established a farm at Newhouse-in-the-Moor in the parish of St Neot towards the end of the twelfth century; Merrifield, near Temple, is recorded in 1241 and Fernacre, in the heart of the moor between Roughtor and Brown Willy, is mentioned in 1327. There were a number of chapels built on the moor in early times. The chapel of St Peter at the source of the Fowey is named in 1239, there was the chapel of St Michael on Roughtor, of St Bellarmin on the tor of that name and St Luke in the upper Fowey valley. These chapels would not have been built unless there were priests to serve them and congregations to hear their masses.

Among the most obvious relics of medieval times found in this area are the granite crosses of which there are more than 350 examples in Cornwall. Every churchyard of Celtic origin had its cross. There is a tenth-century cross-shaft at St Neot and there is also a very fine cross in Cardinham churchyard which is in a particularly good state of preservation because the fifteenth-century church builders incorporated it in the church wall from which it has subsequently been removed. The fact that they did not scruple to use this monument as a piece of building stone indicates that the cross must be an ancient one. A more recent memorial would have been treated with greater respect. The churchyard crosses are probably of early date; those found scattered around the countryside are usually much later. They were erected to mark the trackways across the wastes and to indicate footpaths leading to the parish church. Of the moorland wayside crosses the best known is Fourholes Cross, which stands beside the A30 about a mile west of Bolventor. The four holes of this richly ornamented wheel cross are now two because some local volunteers used it for target practice at the time of the Napoleonic wars, but it is still a very impressive monument in spite of the proximity of a roadside garage built between the two world wars. The course of the trunk road is marked by several other crosses. There is one at Trewint where the moor begins, another at Vincent's Mine near the top of the hill as it rises to Cannaframe and there is Peverell's Cross beside the road as it passes off the moor on its way to Bodmin.

Perhaps the most striking of all the wayside crosses is the Longstone, or Long Tom on Craddock Moor. The monument, which is over 9ft high, stands on a lonely down beside the Redgate-Minions road not far from the Hurlers. The long shaft has a rounded top and on each side of this an oval area has been chipped out, leaving in the centre a Latin cross in bas-relief. This cross, like most of those that mark the trackways, is probably of medieval date but its austere setting, its rough shape and commanding appearance, make it look like a prehistoric menhir. Another remote monument of primitive appearance is the appropriately named Middlemoor Cross which stands beside a track leading from Treswallock past Alex Tor in the direction of Brown Willy. A small farm-house stands about 200yd away and the boundary hedge of its patch of intake runs close beside the cross, but these are comparatively recent developments. Until the nineteenth century this cross must have been surrounded by open down stretching for miles in all directions.

The primitive appearance of many of the wayside crosses is no guarantee of great age and most of these rough-hewn monuments date from medieval times. Nevertheless, some of them are really ancient and the standing stones on which the Christian symbol is hewn may have been erected in pagan times. This is illustrated by an incident described in the *Vita prima Samsonis*, the earliest life of a Celtic saint that we possess, written in the seventh century. The book tells us that Samson, the patron saint of Golant and Southill, sailed from Ireland to the Cornish coast and then, taking his books and sacred vessels with him, set off on a journey. As he was passing through 'a certain district called Tricuria' he came upon a group of people worshipping an idol. Above them on a hill 'an abominable image [was] standing'. On the surface of this the saint chiselled a cross and he destroyed the idol which was the object of their worship. Tricuria is Trigg, a large area in north-west Cornwall which includes the moorland parishes of Blisland, St Breward, Advent and Temple. The story has some very confused elements but it may be something more than legend. Doubtless there are many

86

standing stones in Cornwall, venerated in heathen times, which now have crosses incised on them and it is not impossible that somewhere on Bodmin Moor stands or lies the cross which St Samson sanctified.

Langdon, whose book on Cornish crosses was published in the 1890s, records thirteen in St Breward, eleven in Blisland, eight in Temple, eight in Cardinham, six in Altarnun and five in St Cleer. In St Neot there are eleven known examples, including one at Tredinnick only recently discovered. Inevitably, these monuments have suffered loss and damage through the centuries. Some have been utilised as gateposts and some, like the cross at Tredinnick, have fallen and in course of time have been buried under the soil. Many wayside crosses have been gathered in to the churchyards for their better preservation, but the practice of moving them from one place to another cannot be commended. Many of the crosses are not particularly interesting in themselves; the significant factor is the site where they were originally erected.

Unquestionably of early date are the inscribed stones. Cornwall has many and some of them are sited on the moor. In Cardinham parish there are two which have been removed a few yards from their original position to the crossroads where the road from Mount to Tawna crosses the lane from Welltown to Treslea Downs. The inscriptions, now almost impossible to make out, are *Vailithi fili Urochani*—'(the monument of) Vailithus the son of Urochanus' and *Or(ate) p(ro) Ep(iscopus) Titus*—'Pray for Bishop Titus'. There are no records of Vailithus and no one called Titus has, as far as is known, adorned the bench of bishops. If, indeed, there was such a church dignitary one would have expected that the person who arranged for the setting up of his memorial stone would have had more regard for grammatical accuracy. Perhaps some of the early monumental masons, like their eighteenth-century counterparts, were near-illiterates. There is a stone in St Neot churchyard which gives the word 'memory' three 'm's for good measure.

Most impressive of these inscribed stones is the ornamented

87

cross-base in the parish of St Cleer known as King Doniert's Stone. The inscription, still plainly visible, reads *Doniert rogavit pro anima*—'Doniert has asked (prayers) for his soul'. Close beside it stands a cross-shaft decorated with a pattern of inter-lacing work very similar to the shaft in St Neot churchyard three miles away to the west. This interesting monument was known to the early topographers. Norden mentions it and Carew describes it in some detail:

> There are two moor stones pitched in the ground very near together, the one of a more broad than thick squareness about eight foot in height, resembling the ordinary spill of a cross, and somewhat curiously hewed with diaper work. The other cometh short of his fellow's length by the better half, but well near doub-leth it in breadth and thickness, and is likewise handsomely carved. They both are mortised in the top, leaving a little edge at the one side as to accommodate the placing of somewhat else thereupon.

Doniert is Dungarth—the g is soft as j and can therefore be printed as i. He was the last of the Cornish kings of whom we have any knowledge and was drowned in the Fowey, which runs nearby, in the year 878. Here we are in touch with recorded history; a visit to King Doniert's Stone makes the Dark Ages seem less dark.

Until recent years those who visited the stone had to climb a hedge to get to it. Now the landowner and the Liskeard Old Cornwall Society have combined to set back the hedge so that it is open to the Redgate-Minions road. Half a mile away down the hill is the Fowey where the Cornish king met his death. It is a charming reach of the river. From Draynes Bridge to the cascades of Golitha and beyond, the woods cluster thickly beside it. At most seasons of the year the river runs happily over the shallows and it is hard to believe that it could drown a man, but after heavy rain when it comes roaring down in spate it looks ugly and dangerous.

W. G. V. Balchin suggests that when a warmer and drier climate set in at about AD 500, many of the hill settlements

88

Page 89 (above) The track of the Liskeard–Caradon railway: note the granite sleepers. Picture taken facing north on the flank of Stowe's Hill, looking towards Sharp Tor; *(below)* South Caradon mine. Ruined engine-houses and debris are all that now remains of the richest copper mine in East Cornwall

Page 90 (above) Middle Candra: note the patches of intake. The wheel tracks on the open moor were made by tractors drawing fodder onto the commons for winter feed; *(below)* Roughtor and Stannon claypit: a typical scene in the metamorphic aureole. Note the small fields, the thinly scattered houses, the ruined engine-house and the spread of clay waste, with the beautifully proportioned tor behind

became untenable for lack of water and this resulted in the veneration of natural springs, a cult which was exploited by the early Christian missionaries so that nearly a hundred of these springs are now recorded as holy wells. Most of them are shallow basins fed by springs covered over by a small canopy or well-house which may not be particularly ancient. Dr Thomas Quiller Couch, the father of Q, the novelist and man of letters, made a careful study of many of these wells and intended to write a book upon the subject. In 1894, after his death, his daughters used the material he had collected for their charming *Ancient and Holy Wells of Cornwall* which remains the standard work.

Not surprisingly, only one holy well is recorded on the moor itself. This was at St Bellarmin's Tor above Cardinham where there was also a chapel. The Quiller-Couch sisters reported that there were 'no more distinct traces of masonry than a few stones lying round about', but the remains of a building or enclosure measuring some 90ft ×48ft are still visible and scheduled as an ancient monument as St Bellarmin's Chapel. The area enclosed by dry stone walls, now some 4ft in height, seems rather too large for a medieval chapel sited in such a remote place and may well be a sheep-fold.

Some of the holy wells that lie around the foot of the moor are in excellent condition. There is St Cleer which lies beside the village street. When Thomas Quiller Couch visited it and sketched it in 1850 it was in ruins but enough of the original building remained to enable a satisfactory restoration to be made in 1864. Beside it stands a handsome Latin cross and the well-chapel with the cross that flanks it have, as Betjeman says, 'a look more of Brittany than any other holy well in Cornwall'.

One of the most famous of Cornish holy wells was the well of St Nonna at Altarnun. It was used in former days as a 'bowssening', or ducking well for the cure of madness. There is an often-quoted account by Carew who describes with relish the severe treatment administered to the patient, 'upon which handling, if his right wits returned, St Nunn had the thanks, but if there appeared again small amendment he was bowssened again and again while there remained in him any hope of life for recovery'. The well, which has been in a ruinous condition for 100 years, is now dry because of draining operations in the field to the north-east of the church in which the well is situated.

North of Altarnun is the holy well of St Clether. It is two miles away from the northern boundary of the moor and stands in the lonely remote country between Launceston and Camelford where the enclosed fields are constantly giving place to large stretches of open heath. The lovely valley of the Inney, lined by rocky crags, is essentially a part of this wild country. Here on the northern hillside, remote from human habitation is the well under its canopy, with the baptistry beside it. The Quiller-Couch sisters, writing in 1894, could say, 'through neglect this interesting and beautiful well in its wild and picturesque situation is falling into ruin', but soon after that was written the Reverend S. Baring-Gould undertook the restoration of the baptistry chapel. Writing in the *Cornish Magazine* of December 1898, he describes the situation as he found it:

> Gradually access to the spring became more and more impossible, and all the surrounding ground was converted into a bog. Thorn trees rooted themselves in the crumbling walls and, as they grew, with their strong roots dislodged the stones, and the interior of the chapel became a dense wilderness of brambles set with sharp and rending claws . . . When the pick and spade were brought to work it was ascertained that the chapel was not the original structure of the apostle and founder, but had been constructed in the fifteenth-century . . . The well on the south side was still standing nine feet from the ground and the western door jambs were in place . . . the old stone altar remained in situ. The reconstruction was undertaken in the most conservative spirit. Every stone was replaced whence it had fallen and the only new cut stones introduced were a part of the west window.

The baptistry chapel restored by Baring-Gould stands close to, and slightly below, the little fifteenth-century well-house. The water from the well runs through the chapel, flowing under the rough altar stone on which the consecration crosses are still plainly visible, and passing out through the south wall. These interesting buildings are now enclosed by a fence and most beautifully kept.

Those who discover St Clether find themselves going there again and again, for the place is very hard to resist. Although there is nothing there except, possibly, the altar stone, that is older than the fifteenth century, the remote setting and the wild beauty of the scene take you back to the early days of Celtic Christianity. The well is a mile from the small village and half a mile from the nearest house. As you make your way along the steep hillside towards it, the ancient field hedges and the well-house and restored baptistry provide the only evidence of human settlement. There is nothing else to be seen but the unspoilt valley, the tangle of wild fields and the line of the moor beyond.

Baring-Gould was very active in this part of the country. In *A Book of Cornwall* he writes of 'an ancient British settlement beside Trewartha marsh': 'The houses were long and quadrangular, one was apparently a council chamber, having a judge's seat in granite and benches of granite down the sides. Unfortunately these have been wantonly destroyed recently by a man who was building pigsties.' The account is inaccurate. The destroyed 'council chamber' is unlikely to have been as elaborate as Baring-Gould suggests and the rectangular buildings he describes are more recent than he supposed. Medieval pottery, now in Launceston Museum, has been found there and it is probable that this settlement was built to accommodate the herdsmen who took charge of the cattle brought up to the summer pastures. 'The middle part of the shire,' Carew tells us, 'lieth waste and open, showeth a blackish colour, beareth heath and spiry grass, and serveth in a manner only to summer cattle.' The practice of transferring cattle from lowland regions to the hills during the summer months has continued right down to modern times. During the nineteenth century, arrangements were made to collect cattle at various points in mid-Cornwall, like Mitchell and Summercourt, during the month of May and return them at Michaelmas. An advertisement in the *West Briton* newspaper in 1812 names certain farms and summer pastures in the upper Delank Valley which were to be let and adds, 'there is a dwelling-house for a herd on these premises'.

Mention has been made in previous chapters of the medieval long-houses on Carburrow and Garrow Tor. The most readily accessible of these is the long-house beyond the moor gate that leads out of Tor farmyard on Carburrow. The walls are still about 2ft high and one can see the rectangular shape of the building and the doorways facing each other in the middle of the longer walls. One end of the house would have accommodated the farmer and his family; the other was the byre. It was believed in early days that cattle would thrive best if they could see a fire. They might have been glad enough to do so on Carburrow or Garrow on cold and wet winter nights. On Garrow there are nine rectangular platform houses. They stand on the southern slope of the tor and were all built at right-angles to the contours. The living quarters, which are about 20ft long, have the hearth in the centre and the passages separating house and byre are paved with stone. As these long-houses made provision for the housing of cattle, it is clear that they must have been permanent settlements and not temporary accommodation for the summer herdsmen like the buildings on the edge of Trewartha marsh which Baring-Gould describes. At Carburrow, as we have seen, they were replaced when they became obsolete or ruinous by other buildings on adjacent sites, just as the Hebridean black-houses gave way to more up-to-date dwellings.

Despite the great social gulf between their one-time owners, it might be an appropriate moment to turn from the subject of long-houses to the remains of a more exalted building—the Norman castle at Cardinham. This stands on fairly low ground about a quarter of a mile south-east of the parish church. It was built by Richard Fitz-Turold, the first Lord of Cardinham, just after the Norman Conquest. He had another castle at Week

St Mary in north Cornwall. The castle became ruinous in the fourteenth century and now nothing remains but the outline of the keep on its motte and the bailey. It has been identified with Caadigan which has a place in Arthurian legend, but there was no castle here in Arthur's time. If the Iron Age camp of Bury Castle on the hill above had been reoccupied during the Dark Ages, as Castle Dore near Fowey and Chun Castle in West Penwith were, that would have been a more likely identification.

There are some excellent ancient bridges in this area. Treverbyn which spans the Fowey and Panters Bridge on the Bedalder have already been mentioned. These bridges carry the former main road from Liskeard to Bodmin. In 1412 Bishop Stafford granted an indulgence in favour of Treverbyn Bridge which was rebuilt at that time and Panters Bridge was erected a year or two later. Half-way between these two is St Neot bridge which spans the Loveny. This is an eighteenth-century structure which has lost much of its character in recent years because of necessary widening. Of Altarnun Bridge Henderson, in *Old Cornish Bridges and Streams* (1928), wrote 'An unhappy attempt was made to widen it, with iron girders, in recent years. This has spoilt the beauty of the bridge without greatly increasing its usefulness.' Since the new bridge was built the girders have been removed.

There are two other very fine bridges, one on either side of the moor. Berriow Bridge, which carries the main road from Liskeard to Launceston across the Lynher, dates from the sixteenth century. It was repaired in 1640 and widened on the upper side in 1890. This work was carried out in the same style as the original and the bridge remains an elegant structure, one of the most handsome in the west. On the western side of the moor is Key Bridge, the lowest bridge that crosses the Delank. This is an attractive little sixteenth-century bridge, but the sundial post which stands in the angle of the cutwater is seventeenth century. Key Bridge is the only ancient bridge on this side of the moor because of the destruction wrought by the heavy waterspout which fell on Davidstow Moor on 16 July 1847. This sent a great flood of water down the Camel, breaking down every bridge that spanned it except Helland and Wadebridge, and, as the deluge fell on the watershed, the valley of the Inney received similar treatment and every bridge was destroyed except Trekellearn, which lies to the east of the moorland area. Henderson gives a vivid account of this disaster in *Old Cornish Bridges*, a book which no visitor to the moor should miss.

On the moor itself there are a number of bridges which look more primitive and ancient than those that have been mentioned. These are the clapper bridges, rudely constructed of great blocks of moorstone. They seem closer in spirit to the megalithic age than the nineteenth century from which most of them date. The best examples are on the Delank, the foot-bridge under Butter's Tor and the solid structure at Bedrawle. At Bradford is another, and just before the river tumbles into the Hantergantick gorge is Delphy Bridge, charmingly situated and of ancient appearance, though it is only about seventy years old.

There is much evidence on the moor of man's industrial past. All around the edge of the moor, in the metamorphic aureole which resulted from the altering of the country rock by the heat of the intruded granite, are the relics of man's search for metals. Up to the fifteenth century tin was obtained by streaming, not deep mining. Ore was often discovered on the floors of moorland valleys where it had been deposited in the course of centuries as the result of being washed down from the parent lode higher up the hill. The 'old men', the early tinners, believed that this was a consequence of Noah's Flood and one wonders if that is why that mythical event had a window all to itself in St Neot church. By regulating natural streams to flow over the metalliferous waste, the tinners washed away the lighter and useless residue. They worked their way up the valleys, following the trail of the metal-bearing detritus towards the lode from which the tin-stones and tin-bearing sand had washed away. The visual results of this activity are the grass-grown heaps of waste which choke almost every moorland valley and the trenches, often very deep and wide, which the early tinners excavated. A walk from Bowithick southwards between Bray Down and Buttern Hill reveals this open-cast work very clearly. There is another deep man-made canyon between Bray Down and Leskernick Hill.

The valley in which St Neot stands was the scene of considerable, though intermittent, mining operations during the eighteenth and nineteenth centuries and was typical of all the river valleys leading off the moor. In the Bedalder valley, half a mile to the west of Warleggan Church, a great gash in the hillside marks the ancient Treveddoe or Cabilla Mine, of which, right back at the beginning of the eighteenth century, it was said that it had 'been very much wrought in old time'. Both tin and copper have been taken from it right down to the present century. Between 1901 and 1909 over 2,000 tons of copper ore were mined. There are other mines to the north of Treveddoe, North Wheal Providence started in 1845 and Wheal Esther in 1863.

In 1831 a survey was made for a railway from Wadebridge to Wenford Bridge in the Camel valley, with branches to Bodmin from Dunmere and to Ruthern Bridge from Grogley. To the railway enthusiast this line is of special interest because it was the first standard-gauge railway in Cornwall and, indeed, when it was opened in 1834, there was no steam-worked railway in England nearer than the Midlands. It followed the course of the river and was constructed to carry sea-sand to the farms all the way up the valley. It also carried passengers and was the first line in the country to run excursion trains at cheap rates. On 13 April 1840, it ran an excursion train to Bodmin on the occasion of the public hanging of the brothers Lightfoot who had murdered a Wadebridge man and passengers were able to enjoy the event without leaving their seats! The railway, which is still in use for the transport of china-clay from the Wenford Dries, is one of the most picturesquely sited lines in England as it makes its way down the richly wooded Camel valley. Its construction provided an impetus for mining development on

97

the western side of the moor and in the 1840s several mines were opened. There was Blisland Consols, subsequently re-named Bodmin Moor Consols, and there was Great Mitchell Consols just to the north of St Breward Church. The workings can still be seen close to the road as it reaches its highest point, before descending to the stream which comes down under Hamatethy and Wood Park to the Camel below. Further to the north and well into the moor to the east of Crowdy Reservoir are the burrows of Great Roughtor Consols, a deep mine which yielded both copper and tin. Wheal Bray which lies two and a half miles to the south-east, between Bray Down and Carne Down, was another copper mine opened early in the nineteenth century but it never succeeded in paying off its expenses. It is interesting to note that in 1953 uranium was discovered in the Wheal Bray waste-heaps and trials were carried out by the Atomic Energy Division of the Geological Survey, but these were insufficiently promising to encourage development.

Small-scale mining developments have also been conducted east of the A30 trunk road at Wheal Jane, Wheal Vincent, Wheal Messenger and Halvana Mine and, west of the main road, at Hendra. Horseburrow Shaft was sunk to a depth of 50 fathoms in 1880 and ore taken from the shaft was brought through a tramway tunnel under the main road. This yielded tin, wolfram and arsenic and the mine was being worked as late as 1920. Halvana Mine, according to a prospectus published in 1858 when a new company was formed, was said to have produced £30,000 worth of tin, but this account was probably over-optimistic. During the 1914–18 war 8½ tons of wolfram was produced here.

All these mines were small-scale undertakings and the very existence of some of them would be forgotten were it not for the patient research of A. K. Hamilton Jenkin, whose handbooks on the lesser known mines of Cornwall are invaluable. Most of the mining work undertaken was limited in scope and brought very little profit.

THE MORE RECENT PAST

China-clay was first mined in Cornwall in 1745 on Tregonning Hill near Helston. The Hensbarrow district, as every visitor to Cornwall recognises, has been almost obliterated by this industry. There is plenty of china-clay on Bodmin Moor too, though as it suffers from excessive quantities of 'silver fly'—muscovite or white mica—it lacks the quality of much of the clay produced on Hensbarrow. The first china-clay workings on the moor were at Durford, in the valley that runs under Blisland. Work here started in 1860 to be followed by Carwen, less than a mile away, in 1871. In the valley of the Blisland stream, not far from Durfold and close to the village of Waterloo, could be seen until quite recently the largest water-wheel in England, 50ft in diameter. It was erected in 1913 and by a series of flat rods laid across the moor, for a distance of a mile and a half, it provided power for a water-pump in china-clay workings near Temple. The wheel has now been removed.

The principal evidence of Bodmin Moor's historical past will be found in the south-eastern corner of the moor. In the middle of the nineteenth century the Caradon district was recognised as one of the richest mineral areas in Cornwall. In 1860 there were more than twenty mines in production in this sector of the moor and six of them were paying very good dividends. The greatest and most successful of these mines was South Caradon which struck copper in 1837 at a cost of only £640. During the next thirty-one years it sold ore to the value of £1,128,595 and made a profit of £315,605. By 1883 it had increased the value of the ore raised to well over £1½ million. In that same year the mine was bought by a new company and in the years 1885–6, though copper mining in Cornwall was coming to an end, a further 8,000 tons of ore were raised. But then the mine stopped work because of the rising cost of production and world competition.

During the nineteenth century the output of copper in the Bodmin Moor parishes was 630,000 tons and virtually all of this (600,000 tons) came from the two parishes of St Cleer and Linkinhorne in the Caradon district.

99

It was tremendous while it lasted. South Caradon raised 217,000 tons of ore in some fifty years; Marke Valley, near Upton Cross, produced 128,000 tons in a similar period. Other prolific mines were West Caradon, behind Darite, and Phoenix United, near Minions. They raised just short of 100,000 tons each. Copper mining lasted rather longer in the Caradon area than it did in West Cornwall, but most of its mines stopped working in the 1880s. An exception was Phoenix United which produced tin as well as copper. In 1894 it went into voluntary liquidation but continued in limited production under a receiver. In 1898, however, it closed down and the machinery was sold. By that date the mine had realised £880,000 for tin and half that amount for copper. But in 1908 Phoenix arose from its ashes. With a capital of £100,000 it sank a new shaft and a large engine-house, still standing, was built. Work stopped at the beginning of the 1914–18 war and when the war was over it was hoped to start again with the help of a government grant, but nothing came of it. So the last of the great undertakings came to an end. Now the whole area has reverted to moorland once again.

If you turn into the rough lane beside the Methodist Church in the old mining hamlet of Crow's Nest, a walk of less than half a mile brings you into the heart of the old copper country. The lane leads up into a narrow valley at the head of which is the source of the Seaton river. It is a peaceful spot today with no living thing in sight except for the cattle grazing along the grassy banks of the infant stream. But above you, on the steep slopes of the ravine, is a scene of dereliction. The moor is covered with spoil heaps, innumerable paths and roadways and gaunt ruined engine-houses and other stone buildings that were teeming with activity a century ago. As you come up to the moor the lane passes under a bridge which carries the embankment of the old Liskeard and Caradon railway. In the very early days of copper mining in this area transport was a considerable problem, for the roads from Caradon to Liskeard were narrow and hilly and almost impassable in bad weather. So a railway was designed to run from Moorswater, below Liskeard, up into the hills to serve the profitable mines of South and West Caradon and the Cheesewring quarry beyond. The quarry, and Wheal Phoenix adjacent to it, were reached by an inclined plane with a gradient of 1 in 11; this can still be traced up the gully past Gonamena. The line came into full use in 1846. At first the loaded waggons came down to Moorswater by gravity and were brought back to the moor by horses. From Moorswater the mineral ore and granite were taken to Looe by way of the Liskeard and Looe Union Canal, opened in 1828. This canal proved unable to cope with the traffic when the Caradon mines were at the peak of their production and it was replaced by a railway which was constructed for the most part in the canal bed. This line was opened in 1862 and locomotives replaced the horses for the conveyance of freight to and from the mines. The mineral line was then extended from Tokenbury Corner around the eastern side of Caradon to the Cheesewring quarry so that the steep Gonamena incline went out of use. A branch line (its course is still visible) ran over Langstone Downs to serve the granite quarry on Kilmar.

In 1881 the line was extended northwards across the moor along the western side of the Witheybrook. This was the time when everybody was enthusiastic about railways and the intention was to extend the line to the North Cornwall Railway between Launceston and Camelford. But the collapse of the mines in the Caradon area because of the falling price of copper put an end to this project and in 1886 the railway company became bankrupt and the work on the extension stopped. It is possible now to follow the track from Tokenbury Corner, past Minions and Stowe's Hill, along the marshy valley of the Witheybrook into the remote moor and find the most northerly point the railway reached. You feel a little like Parnesius in Kipling's *Puck of Pook's Hill* when he came to Hadrian's Wall: 'I could see the statue not a quarter of a mile away and there I went. At some time or other the Great North Road ran under it into Valentia; but the far end had been blocked up because of the Picts and on the plaster a man had scratched "Finish!" ' The track runs into a cutting and then stops. Beyond it is country which is as lonely and desolate today as the land beyond Hadrian's Wall in the time of the Roman occupation—the marshes of the Witheybrook, the boulders on the summits of Carey Tor and Fox Tor, the wide downs of East Moor and the bogs of Redmire.

The railway continued in use as far as the Cheesewring until well into the present century, but the transport of granite and mineral ores, rapidly diminishing in quantity, was insufficient to make it a viable proposition. It was closed in 1917 and the rails were lifted.

Unlike the mines further to the west on the perimeter of the moor, the undertakings in the Caradon district employed a great many people. Most of the villages that cluster thickly round the south-eastern corner of the moor are nineteenth-century creations. At the peak of their prosperity, which varied in date from mine to mine, South Caradon, West Caradon and Phoenix United each employed over 500 persons; East Caradon and Craddock Moor had 250 workers and several other mines each employed over 100 men. At the beginning of the nineteenth century the population of the parish of St Cleer was 774; this had risen to just short of four thousand by 1861. But a heavy price was paid for the prosperity of the district in terms of human life. In the second decade of the century the parish registers reveal that the average age at death was 48 years 1 month. Forty years later the figure was 21 years 6 months. The Reverend J. R. Prettyman Berkeley who was vicar of St Cleer in the middle of the century estimated that a miner who started work at the age of 15 had only 17 years' expectation of life compared with 31 years, for those who took up other occupations. The miner's work was, of course, difficult and dangerous. The long ladders which had to be climbed at the end of the day's work laid a great strain on the heart and the change from the stifling heat of the underground workings to the damp, cool moorland atmosphere was the cause of a variety of lung complaints. But the chief reason for early death was the poor living standard, the bad housing, the indifferent and inadequate food. Wages were low, even at the best of times, and when the mines began to fail the situation became desperate. There was much emigration to the mines in other parts of the world and for many years families in Pensilva and St Cleer and the surrounding settlements were dependent on the help they received from their kith and kin in foreign lands. We find evidence of this today. Every summer the visitor's books of the local churches record the names of strangers with Cornish names who come from America, Australia and South Africa. They are the descendants of emigrants driven out by the failure of the mines three generations ago, visitors who have come on pious pilgrimage.

Here, round Caradon, the evidence of our industrial past is more evident than it is in the sheltered valleys of the southern and western fringes of the moor. The district is undergoing change. The old mining settlements are rapidly losing their original character because of building development and this corner of the moor with its many archaeological sites is frequently visited, but it retains its atmosphere, a curious blend of romantic wildness and industrial squalor. These contrasting elements are vividly portrayed by Wilkie Collins in *Rambles Beyond Railways* which describes a visit to Cornwall in the mid-nineteenth century. Of his journey across the moor to visit the Cheesewring he says:

We had been walking hitherto amid almost invariable silence and solitude; but now, with each succeeding minute, strange, mingled, unintermitting noises began to grow louder and louder around us. We followed a sharp curve in the tram-way, and immediately found ourselves saluted by an entirely new prospect, and surrounded by an utterly bewildering noise. All about us monstrous wheels were turning slowly; machinery was clanking and groaning in the hoarsest discords; invisible waters were pouring onward with a rushing sound; high above our heads, on skeleton platforms, iron chains clattered fast and fiercely over iron pulleys, and huge steam pumps puffed and gasped, and slowly raised and depressed their heavy black beams of wood. Far beneath the embankment on which we stood, men, women, and children were breaking and washing ore in a perfect marsh of copper-coloured mud and copper-coloured water. We had penetrated to the very centre of the noise, the bustle, and the population on the surface of a great mine.

When we walked forward again, we passed through a thick plantation of young firs; and then, the sounds behind us became slowly and solemnly deadened the further we went on. When we had arrived at the extremity of the line of trees, they ceased softly and suddenly. It was like a change in a dream.

As you walk over the moor, where the relics of the past are so thickly spread, you become aware not only of the layers of history reaching back into the past, but also of the universality of the moor. Man comes and builds his house and clears his fields, he drives his crowbar into the living rock, he digs out the leat and sinks the shaft. Conditions change, the work is abandoned and the moor takes over, laying its patina over the work of man's hands so that all this evidence of human chronology is reduced to the same timelessness. On the eastern slope of Brown Willy, just below the summit, is a circular hut still partially roofed with stone slabs. It could be the work of Bronze Age man or it could be only 100 years old. The clapper bridges that span the Delank at Butter's Tor and Bedrawle look as primitive as Trethevy Quoit, yet they were probably built in the last century. Despite the 2,000 years that separate the stone ramparts above the Cheesewring from the ruined buildings of West Phoenix Mine less than a mile away, one is aware only of their similarities. They blend together into the natural scene. Bronze Age farmer, Iron Age warrior, medieval herdsman and tin streamer, and nineteenth-century miner have all gone, leaving their traces behind them, and as we walk about and see the evidence of what they were and what they accomplished, time seems to be foreshortened. The spirit of the moor has absorbed them and made them one.

5   THE PRESENT

FOR the visitor to the moor, Sheet 186 of the one-inch edition of the Ordnance Survey map or the new metric sheets 200 and 201 are essential. Not only should a map be his constant companion on moorland walks, it can also provide him, as W. G. Hoskins pointed out in his delightful book *The Making of the English Landscape*, with hours of pleasure and imaginative excitement if he will sit down and read it like a book. He will also profit from a study of the six-inch sheets because these reveal the field lay-out and the settlement pattern. As is to be expected, the enclosed lands lie around the edge of the moor and along the river valleys. Enclosed fields border the Fowey right up into the heart of the moor beyond the A30 trunk road and the Delank valley has been settled as far as Fernacre and Maiden Tor. The enclosures around Bolventor, in the centre of the moor, are the result of the enterprise of a local landowner.

Between these settled areas there are numerous stretches of unenclosed land and most of these are lands on which there are rights of common. Rather more than 17,000 acres, between a third and a half of the moorland area, is common land. There is a large unfenced region in the north-west, stretching from Davidstow Moor eastwards past Buttern Hill to Bray Down, an area which includes Roughtor, Leskernick Hill and Tolborough Tor, and another, a long strip on the eastern side of the moor which takes in East Moor, Trewortha, Hawk's Tor, Kilmar, Langstone Downs, Stowe's Hill, Caradon and Craddock Moor. These are lands that carry rights of common and so do Shallow Water and Brocklebarrow, Manor Common,

Trehudreth Downs and Cardinham Moor. There are also some isolated patches of common in the south—Penkestle and the adjoining Letter Moor, Goonzion and Draynes Common in St Neot and Treslea and Tawna in Cardinham.

The right of common has been defined as 'a right, which one or more persons may have, to take or use some portion of that which another man's soil naturally produces'. The origin of this right is ancient and obscure. It dates back to the day of the medieval manor which was a self-contained unit consisting not only of areas of cultivated land, but also of waste which was used for pasturage and the gathering of fuel. Without these rights it would have been impossible for the peasantry to live and the Lord of the Manor could not enclose common land and prevent the commoners from exercising their rights without the authority of parliament.

In medieval times it was not only the waste that was un-enclosed, but also the large areas of arable land on which the Lord of the Manor and his tenantry cultivated separate un-fenced strips, managed in a uniform manner by mutual consent. Enclosure, a gradual and continuous process, was due mainly to changes in agricultural practice that brought about the collapse of the old open-field system. The process was particularly rapid in the eighteenth century when arable farming was being revolutionised and when members of parliament were predominantly landed gentry, sympathetic to the needs of their own kind. Enclosure, though catastrophic for the peasantry, greatly increased agricultural productivity, but the importing of cheap food in the mid-nineteenth century and the growth of the urban population brought about a new conception of the importance of common land which, in urban areas, began to be used for recreational purposes and the rate of enclosure slowed down.

Enclosure has also taken place since the earliest times by a colonising process, the taming of the wild by the breaking and fencing of uncultivated land. It is this process that has been responsible for the enclosures on Bodmin Moor. The Domesday

Page 107 (above) Altarnun: a view of the handsome church across the ancient bridge which was clumsily widened in the last century. It has now been converted to a footbridge; (below) St Cleer Well was carefully restored in the middle of the last century. Note the modern bungalow development in the distance

Page 108 (above) Bedrawle Bridge: a rough clapper bridge built of heavy granite blocks which carries a farm track across the Delank; (below) St Neot village from Goonzion Downs: the holy well is under the trees in the flat meadow on the left of the picture

survey reveals that virtually the whole of the moor consisted of manorial waste. The manor of Fawton contained an area of pasture measuring seven miles by four, Liscarret (Liskeard) had pasture that was four miles by two, and Henliston (Helstone in Trigg) three miles by two. The wastes of these three manors alone covered over forty square miles, more than half the moorland area. Although the more fertile and sheltered lands were enclosed and settled from the twelfth century onwards, there were very large expanses of open pasture used in common. We do not know how the rights of common were apportioned in early times. On Dartmoor, early records show that in the thirteenth century the moor provided common grazing for virtually all the inhabitants of Devon who wished to make use of it. No doubt the rights of pasturage on Bodmin Moor were widely extended. In his parish history of St Neot, Michell has a passage which seems to imply that rights of common were at one time determined on a parochial basis. 'The owners of the adjoining lands in Alternun,' he says, 'have, by repeated trespasses, possessed themselves of upwards of six hundred acres of common and marsh land . . . belonging to St Neots, thus despoiling the parish of a considerable tract of land.'

Through the centuries rights of common have been eroded in a number of ways. If Michell's statement is accurate there has been large-scale appropriation of land in the remote parts of the moor and the present disposition of common lands reveals that there are a number of 'islands' of land, on which there are no common rights, surrounded by large areas of common. Smith's Farm on East Moor is an example; Leskernick, a small isolated farmhouse backed by three fields on the eastern bank of the upper Fowey is another, and the long strip of common land along the eastern edge of the moor is broken by the village of Henwood and the adjacent farms and also by the mining village of Minions. Some of these settlements and their small pockets of land may be the result of mining development, others may have been established by squatting rights—

the custom which enabled a man to lay claim to common land by putting up a shed or house overnight, and ensuring that smoke was issuing from its chimney before daybreak.

The pasturing of stock on common land is, as we shall see, an essential part of the farming economy of Bodmin Moor at the present time. Rights of common are limited to the occupants of certain farms and the large area of common land—more than thirty square miles—is administered by the well-organised and active Cornwall Commoners' Association.

It was formerly a condition of the award of the hill cattle subsidy that a third of it should be spent on the improvement of the land and the money allocated for this purpose was administered by the Commoners' Association through local committees. This is no longer the practice and the farmer receives the subsidy in full. It was never a popular arrangement because, naturally enough, each farmer preferred to spend his subsidy in his own way and also because many of them were opposed to the 'improvement' of the unenclosed land. The treatment of the moor with lime and fertilisers had the effect of destroying the pervasive purple moor grass and encouraging the growth of the bent and fescue species. The purple moor grass was useful for winter grazing because, though its nutritive value is limited, it fills the bellies of the cattle and provides a valuable addition to the daily ration of hay brought to them on the ground. The grasses developed by the application of fertilisers were eaten close to the ground in the summer and there was a tendency for mosses to grow in their place. The improvement of the moor is regarded as worthwhile only in enclosed areas which can be cleared of stock as appropriate.

An attempt has been made in recent years to clear up the obscurity that exists with regard to rights of common. The Common Registration Act of 1965 has prescribed the registration of all common rights. The final date for doing this was in January, 1970. All registered rights to which no objections had been raised by 31 July 1972, were deemed to have been established and those that have been challenged are now under review. It is important to remember that common land is private property, it is not in public ownership. Although access to commons has been customary, the general public have no more legal right to enter them than they have to invade a stranger's back garden. The commons are owned as all land is, and the only difference between them and other lands is that certain persons, by virtue of their occupancy of certain holdings, enjoy specified rights to the product of their soil. If you walk on Bodmin Moor except on a public highway or registered footpath you do so without legal justification. 'Jus spatiandi' (the right to wander) was disallowed in a court case in 1905 in which the plaintiff claimed the right of walking around Stonehenge which was then privately owned. The court decided against him.

Common of pasture is virtually the only form of common right now exercised on the moor but there are others, including the right of turbary (the right to dig turf). This used to be of great importance. A moorland walk today is unlikely to bring to the nostrils the pungent reek of peat smoke, for the harvesting of peat is such a long and laborious process that in these days it is seldom undertaken. Thirty years ago, almost every farmhouse in the centre of the moor was flanked by a peat stack almost as high as the house itself and the farm kitchen had an open hearth in which to burn it. One wonders how many of those who live on Bodmin Moor have taken the trouble to register their rights of turbary, for the rising cost of coal and oil may encourage them to exercise those rights again.

In the past common lands might not be enclosed without ministerial consent, which was only given if the enclosure was for the benefit of the neighbourhood. A recent example of this is the fencing of the main trunk road from the commons which border it on the north-western side continuously from Bolventor to the southern boundary of the moor. The commoners gave up land for the purpose and contributed towards the cost. The provision of this fencing was to the advantage of the stock holder and the motorist, but the conversion of the road to a dual carriageway has created problems. When this development was designed the existence of the commons, possibly because they were already fenced off, seems to have been overlooked and the construction of underpasses was not considered. The A30 is bordered by Brockabarrow Common, Manor Common, Trehudreth Downs and Cardinham Moor and it so happens that the homesteads of most of the farmers with common rights are separated from their grazing grounds by the main road. The construction of underpasses, made difficult because the two roadways are sometimes at different levels, is unlikely to be undertaken in the near future and temporary expedients must be devised to enable the commoners to exercise their rights.

As we have seen, since early times the moor has been chiefly used for the pasturing of cattle, but though the traditional pastoral economy still prevails, Bodmin Moor has felt the effect of the changes in agricultural practice that have come about during the last half-century. This can be tested by walking over the moor today and talking to a few farmers and then, in contrast, by picking up Margaret Leigh's very readable account of her experience of farming on Bodmin Moor some forty years ago. The book takes us into a different world. In 1935, almost the worst year in the century for the British farmer, she signed a seven-year lease for the little holding of Newton on the edge of Trehudreth Downs in the parish of Blisland. The farm consisted of forty-four acres of enclosed land with an unlimited moor right, which she obtained at a rental of less than £40 per annum. There was no electricity, water was drawn from the well, there was a peat fire. The farm work consisted of a little of everything. Pigs were raised, sheep were kept; though the farmhouse was some distance from a metalled road and linked with it by a rutted track over the down, milk was produced and laboriously conveyed to the stand every morning. She cut corn in her steeply sloping 3-acre field with the scythe; she had a neighbour who kept his money in a pot buried in one of his fields. Anachronistic though this sounds there were plenty of moorland farms of similar pattern in the 1930s and even during the war. Milk was produced under the most unlikely conditions and its daily transport to the collection point might well involve a journey over roadless waste and the crossing of an unbridged ford or two. All the scattered homesteads from Brown Willy to Brown Gelly and from Hendra Beacon to Trehudreth Downs, burned turf, and on many of them the cooking was done in the traditional way on a baking iron under an inverted pan smothered with peat embers. The war made its impact, of course. The tiny windows were covered with black-out curtains which contained the heat as well as the light of the Aladdin lamp, the air was thick with the drone of aircraft, the commoners spent much time moving their cattle before firing practice with live ammunition sent the shells hurtling across the sky from Siblyback to High Moor. The traditional practice of feeding oats in the sheaf to the cattle had largely to be discontinued and threshing machines penetrated to rick yards where they had never been seen before. I recall a bright winter day when the thresher came to Codda for the first time in the history of that ancient homestead. There are few mechanical devices that look more primitive than the old threshing unit, the steam engine, thresher and elevator, but as this cumbersome apparatus made its way along the boulder-strewn track, negotiating the awkwardly placed gateways bounded by granite posts like prehistoric menhirs, it seemed a modern intrusion. It took half a day to get into position.

Those days are over. The farmsteads that have not been abandoned are linked to the outside world with good roads. The old peasant smallholder is no longer found on the moor and the average size of a moorland farm is now over 180 acres.

The hill farms are much more heavily stocked than they used to be. The moor is no longer an area whose chief function is the summer pasturage of cattle, for stock run on the downs all the year round. A study of the six-inch sheet of the Ordnance Survey map reveals that the increased productivity of the hill farms has affected the field pattern. If you compare the map with the situation as you find it on the ground, you find a noticeable difference, for many farmers are drastically reducing the number of their hedges. The shape and size of the fields was originally determined in moorland areas by the amount of surface stone which had to be removed from them and the enclosures were often extremely small, 2 acres or less. A complex of tiny fields is not well adapted to modern farming conditions. Now that production is intensified and the farms more heavily stocked, the small fields are inadequate. Gateways are too narrow for present-day farm machinery and the number of animals too large to be accommodated in the fields as originally designed. If gates are removed so that stock have the run of several fields the gateways can become almost impassable during the winter months. Under present conditions a farm is more economically and efficiently managed if it is divided into fairly large units. The removal of the stone walls covered with turf which serve for hedges in Cornwall, a simple operation with modern equipment, can increase the effective acreage of a farm by as much as 5 per cent. It is worth noting that the elimination of the small fields, unless it is done with landscaping as well as agricultural needs in mind, can be a process destructive of amenity. Besides, the original field pattern of a farm is an historical document. Reshaping it is like pulling down an ancient building and erecting another in its place, so the six-inch map becomes a valuable record.

Increasing production is also responsible for the greater use of the open moor during the winter months. If all the cattle were brought home and turned loose in the enclosed fields in this area of heavy rainfall the land would be trampled out of existence. Scarcity of labour and its cost, together with the expense of putting up the necessary buildings, discouraged the practice of housing cattle in the winter though some farmers do. Rather less than a third of the stock on moorland farms spend the winter under cover. Cattle do well on the open down where they have a healthier and more profitable existence and cost the farmer less. Cattle cannot, of course, live off the land in wintertime and food must be taken to them. Up till six weeks before calving the cow requires from 17 to 20lb of hay each day according to quality and for the last six weeks, and to the end of the first month of lactation, the hay ration must be increased and other food added. The ration must be supplemented again after that until the spring and the rejuvenation of the pastures.

There are approximately 10,000 cows on Bodmin Moor and they spend a great deal of the year on unenclosed ground. They are brought back to the homestead soon after they have calved which is usually in the early months of the year. Routine injections are then administered and the bull calves are gelded. Gradually, as the calves are born the stock is brought down from the hills and by the end of April almost all will have calved. The bulls run with the herd in the home pastures in the spring, and in early summer the cows with their calves beside them are returned to the commons. Weaning is a gradual and natural process and the calves are disposed of in the autumn sales, the moor farmer's harvest time. In the summer hay or silage is taken from the enclosed lands in preparation for the winter. If corn is grown as a part of the process of rotation it is often cut and baled, like hay, just as it begins to change colour.

It is not possible to finish a beef animal for the butcher on a moorland farm and the usual practice is to sell the calves in the first year, though some are retained until they are eighteen-months old. Bulls may not be turned loose on the commons and unless a farmer has fenced hill lands not subject to common rights, he cannot take the bulls to the herd on the downs. There is very little land on the high moor which fulfils these conditions, so the general practice is to bring the cows back to the enclosed land around the farmsteads for service.

The suckler-cow industry demands a considerable acreage for its financial success, so there is a tendency for small farms, as they come into the market, to be absorbed into larger units. Farmers who occupy the few smallholdings that remain have to supplement their income in various ways. Some undertake contract work, hay-baling, potato-lifting and the like. Others add to their living through the tourist trade by the provision of camping sites and by letting accommodation. Pony-trekking is also gaining ground. In 1972 it was estimated that about 140 horses on moorland farms were available for hire. This activity, and the modern cult of horse-riding, is responsible for the large number of horses and ponies seen on the commons, particularly on the western side of the moor. The moorland farmers who stick to cattle do not welcome this development, for horses are voracious feeders and poach the ground heavily in winter. On the western side of the area and on Davidstow Moor there are also a great number of sheep. On the eastern side cattle predominate. Under modern conditions the small farmer cannot hope to make an adequate living on the moor by traditional farming methods alone. Fifty or sixty years ago he was virtually self-supporting and content to accept a standard of living and a way of life peculiar to the area, but those days will not return.

The existence of nearly 18,000 acres of common land on Bodmin Moor is vital to the farming economy and it determines the nature of the area. The modern moorland farm is no longer a peasant holding cut off from the outside world by its physical remoteness and its different way of life. It now has good road communications and electric power. Every farm-house now occupied is only a few minutes by car from its nearest country town, Camelford, or Bodmin, or Launceston, or Liskeard. But though its annual cycle of work is affected by modern agricultural developments, it is committed to a traditional farming economy. The modern moorland farmer produces beef cattle as his Bronze Age predecessors did.

There are only ten English counties which have a greater acreage of common lands than Cornwall and of these, all except Devon, Hampshire and Surrey are in the north. More than three-quarters of the area of Cornish common land is on Bodmin Moor and this determines the fact that it contains the largest amount of open space in the county. Although, as has been explained, the general public have no legal right of access to this open area, the presence of pedestrians and horsemen on the commons has, hitherto, been tolerated. The future of the area is somewhat uncertain because the moor is under immense pressures. The problem will be discussed at some length in the concluding chapter, but the importance of these open spaces cannot be overestimated. They play a necessary rôle in current farming practice and preserve a link with the past. To the growing number of people who are apprehensive about some aspects of modern agricultural development, farming on the moor as it is now conducted is a matter for satisfaction. The moorland farmer does not go in for intensive 'factory' methods, or mono-cropping, or the heavy and exclusive use of artificial fertilisers. The farmyard slurry does not go down the drain but back onto the land. Some moor farmers believe that the moors are too heavily stocked and that the practice of running the cattle on the moor in winter is bad husbandry, a policy that makes for quantity rather than quality. They regard it as more efficient to raise a smaller number of cattle on enclosed land. Now that as a result of the registration of common rights the commoners are identifiable, it may become possible for hill land to be fenced and improved by mutual consent of the commoners. This point of view is naturally more common in areas where the hill pastures are over-stocked. In many parts of the moor the open areas can easily accommodate the stock that graze them. Although the ground is poached in winter near the feeding places and the herbage is eaten down to the roots, the cattle run free and manure the ground from which they draw their sustenance. Because the commons exist, beef cattle can be raised in natural, free-range conditions and the town dweller can refresh his spirit by the sight of land on which the hand of man lies very lightly.

Apart from agriculture the principal activity on the moor today is the extraction of china-clay. As we have seen, this valuable product is the result of the decomposition of the feldspar in the granite. It was first produced in Germany in the early years of the eighteenth century and it was in 1745 that William Cookworthy first found china-clay on the western side of Tregonning Hill, near Helston. The industry grew rapidly and in the century from 1827 to 1929 the annual yield increased from 11,000 tons to 869,000 tons. After World War II the industry underwent great changes, for it was in serious need of modernisation. Up to 1939 most of the work was still being done by hand, and in 1945 the overburden was still removed with pick and shovel and the clay dried by the wasteful kiln method instead of by filter press.

Production of china-clay began on Bodmin Moor in 1860 and during the next twenty years a number of small pits were opened, chiefly on the southern and western edges of the moor. The clay is inferior in quality to that produced in the St Austell area and in the early days there were considerable transport problems. Nevertheless there has been a good deal of this industrial activity in the area. At the time of writing the extensive clayworks at Stannon and Parson's Park are the only ones in operation on the moor.

A visit to a china-clay pit today reveals how thoroughly this industry has been mechanised, for the labour force is minute in comparison to the scale of the undertaking. One may stand on the edge of a great pit or quarry 150ft deep and more than 300ft across and see only two or three men at work. There may be a caterpillar tractor employed in grading the sides of the pit or breaking down the lumps of clay, work that used to be done by hand, and there will be a man in charge of the engine that operates the pump; another will be supervising the automatic hoses, or monitors, that wash out the clay. In the vast amphitheatre there may well be no other human being in sight. The sloping sides of the pit reveal rock with a variety of texture. Beneath a dark band, 10–15ft in depth, from which the overburden has been removed, the slopes mainly consist of coarse sand, off-white in colour. Here and there are areas of slightly darker and more solid rock insufficiently disintegrated to yield to attack from the powerful jets of water delivered by the monitors, though exposure to the weather will eventually break them down and this process can be expedited by the caterpillar tractors. The area is punctuated by a number of solid granite boulders which from time to time are bull-dozed into heaps and removed from the pit.

The slurry washed down by the hoses collects at the bottom of the pit and is pumped to ground level. Although it looks like liquid milk it contains a very high proportion of solids, and you can hear the noise of the constant bombardment of granite particles against the side of the pipe as it is drawn to the surface. When the slurry reaches the top of the pit it is pounded and agitated by mechanical means and the sand is conveyed to the top of the burrow or waste heap by conveyor belt. Formerly the burrows were higher and more conical than they are today, and the spoil was taken up in trucks. The creamy-looking mixture that remains is subjected to a series of processes and passes through a number of settling tanks in which the waste products sink to the bottom and the clay is held in suspension. At this stage of production chemicals are added to whiten the clay and make it more buoyant in the settling tank so that it is more easily separated from the micaceous waste. Samples of the slurry are analysed each day to determine the nature of the chemical treatment.

Finally, the china-clay from which the impurities have been removed, runs by gravity through pipes to the 'dries' which stand beside the railway and may be several miles away from the point where the clay is quarried. The china-clay from Stannon is dried at Wenford in the Camel valley and the clay from Parson's Park goes to Moorswater below Liskeard. After it is dried the product is railed to Par or Fowey for ship-ment. The micaceous waste from the settling tanks is pumped into large lagoons adjoining the workings. Most of the water used in washing out the clay and conveying it to ground level is eventually returned to the bottom of the pit to be used again.

Between 80 and 90 per cent of the material removed is waste. About three-quarters of it is piled on the burrows and has some value for road-making and for the construction of building blocks. The spoil heaps of the china-clay works at Hawk's Tor, beside the main road, are now used for this purpose and some of the waste from Parson's Park is utilised in the same way, but the transport of this bulky material creates a problem. The micaceous waste in the lagoon contains too much liquid to make it of commercial value and constitutes an embarrassment to the industry and an affront to the conservationist. At Parson's Park, for instance, about 100,000 tons of this waste are deposited every year. At once time the effluent was discharged into the rivers; the waste from Stannon pit went down through the gorge of the Devil's Jump to the Camel below Trecarne, and the Parson's Park works polluted the Loveny. What happens now is less objectionable and the damage to the environment is at least localised. Nevertheless, it is a most disquieting feature in this form of industrial development. The pyramidal spoil heaps do not seriously disfigure the landscape—they even have a bizarre beauty of their own—but the lagoons of micaceous waste are a menace, stretching out across the countryside, burying prehistoric remains and plant life, and destroying the natural contours of the ground. Eventually, perhaps, when the moisture has evaporated and pits become worked out, the contents of the lagoons and the sand ramps that contain them will be tipped back into the quarries whence they came, but in the meantime they will sterilise the land for many decades. A visit to Stannon can be a horrifying experience. China-clay has been produced here for a long time but developments have been particularly extensive in recent years. Stannon farmhouse, an attractive L-shaped building, is now almost completely surrounded by great ramps of sand enclosing creamy lakes of waste, which reach out into an area rich in prehistoric remains and in close proximity to the most impressive hill on the moor. No one who stands by the Stannon stone circle and looks towards Roughtor can feel anything but unhappy.

Fortunately, however, the dirt is 'clean' dirt and when workings are abandoned nature soon takes over. Broom bushes are flourishing on the upper slopes of the clay pit at Parson's Park and self-sown grass and other herbage has already started to establish itself. The industry is experimenting successfully in encouraging the growth of vegetation on the spoil heaps but, economic considerations apart, this highly developed and successful industry is an undesirable intrusion in an area of such great natural beauty.

Granite has been an important building material for thousands of years. Bronze and Iron Age man used the moorstone for the purpose and the medieval church-builders found an adequate supply of stone on the surface, but quarrying has continued for a considerable time. Granites are of different kinds. The finer types of granite are the result of more rapid cooling or of greater acidity, a characteristic of the later intrusions. The Cornish granites are coarser than those found in other parts of Britain, but those which are finest in texture occur in the neighbourhood of Dozmary Pool and near the edges of the moor, particularly on the west. The finer granites in the centre of Bodmin Moor are later intrusions and this probably accounts for the comparatively smooth terrain. Because of the finer texture of the granite and the transport problem, most of the granite quarries are situated near the moor's edge. The smaller quarries, with the exception of Bearah Tor, are no longer worked, for the high cost of modern production requires a large capital outlay. Granite is now produced on a large scale only in the lower valley of the Delank at Hantergantick and Delank quarries.

At Delank the quarries are now about 150ft deep. The rock is broken out by pneumatic drills into large blocks which are hoisted to the surface by crane. The blocks are sawn into pieces of appropriate size and shape by wire saws, electrically powered. The wire revolves rapidly around the block and the cutting process is achieved by washing carborundum powder into the cuts under pressure. Greater precision can be obtained by the use of diamond saws, some of which operate automatically. The machine is set and the saws, two of them working side by side, move slowly backwards and forwards through the block which may be several feet thick. The polishing of the granite is also an electrically powered and automatic process, though finer and more intricate work is carried out by the control of hand-operated power-driven polishers. The bulk of the work now undertaken is the preparation of stones for the monumental mason, though building blocks and veneers are also manufactured and stone blocks of complicated pattern, precisely measured to a fraction of an inch, are also prepared for certain kinds of industrial use. The accuracy of the work on such resistant material is amazing. It is possible to cut a granite block which weighs several tons into slabs each less than an inch thick, so that when the operation is completed the stone resembles a sliced loaf.

The Delank quarry has been in operation for more than 100 years. The 1859 edition of *Murray's Handbook for Travellers in Devon and Cornwall* describes 'the deep romantic valley' of Hantergantick and adds, 'A few years ago Hanter-Gantick was as solitary as it is wild, but it is now the site of granite-works.' From the canyons chiselled laboriously out of the side of the Delank valley came the blocks which built the Eddystone lighthouse and the Smeaton tower that preceded it, several of the Thames bridges, and the Cenotaph in Whitehall. When one recalls that a cubic foot of granite weighs 1½cwt and that all the cutting and shaping of the stone was done by hand, one realises the immensity of the undertaking. The weight of this material makes transport costly and difficult. Up to the time of World War II much of the Delank granite was transported by rail. There was a steep incline from the railhead at Wenford Bridge to the granite quarries. Now the finished material is conveyed by road and the incline has been demolished.

Before the quarry was connected to the national grid it harnessed the Delank and did much of its work by hydraulic power, which is still used to supplement electricity. Above the quarry the river is directed into a pipe for the purpose. But this intense industrial activity has done surprisingly little to disfigure the magnificent valley. *Murray's Guide* describes this place with considerable enthusiasm:

It is a scene befitting the genius of a Salvator, and one of the most extraordinary of its kind in the country. The declivity of the higher part of the valley is abrupt, and here the stream thunders through the obstruction in a series of cascades. A descent to its banks will repay the labour, although a ladder is almost required in the passage from stone to stone, and a thick growth of brake offers additional impediments.

It all looks very much like that today. The thick growth of brake is still present, hiding the industrial development.

The Delank is a moorland river for almost every inch of its course and there is no wilder scene on the moor than that which borders it in its final descent to Key Bridge and the valley pastures where it joins the Camel. When the river emerges from the pipe beside the quarries it rushes down a boulder-strewn bed, rich in autumn with the festoons of rowan berries that overhang it. The outline of the little hills above is broken by numerous craggy tors and in the industrial area the abandoned cuttings, stained with iron oxide, now look almost as wild as the natural scene in which they are found. Hantergantick is still a place of great beauty.

Tourism, regarded as Cornwall's most important industry has made little impact on Bodmin Moor until recent years. 'Mountains which are quite barren with scarce a tree or hedge' is how an unknown diarist who crossed the moor in 1795 describes it, and he was glad when the country changed 'to a beautiful scene' in the neighbourhood of Bodmin. In *Rambles Beyond Railways* (1851) the novelist, Wilkie Collins, writes of a visit to the St Cleer antiquities and gives a vivid and horrific account of his overnight accommodation at a Liskeard inn where the landlady, 'looking very thin and careworn and clad in mourning weeds' regaled him and his companion on 'some rugged lumps of broiled flesh', and where they spent the evening in a room 40ft long furnished with 'six immense wooden tables, painted of a ghastly yellow colour. Nothing was placed on any of them—they looked like dissecting-tables waiting for "subjects" '. Collins and his friend sat at another smaller table 'covered with crape and bombazine' by the light of one candle brought by a servant who 'desired to be informed whether we wanted two sheets apiece to our beds or whether we could do with a sheet at top and a blanket at bottom, as other people did'. Clearly, Liskeard made no concessions to tourism in the mid-nineteenth century. J. H. Wade in his *Rambles in Cornwall* (1928) devoted one brief chapter to Bodmin Moor which he describes as being well off the track of the tourist and difficult to explore, and Claude Berry in *Portrait of Cornwall* (1963) wonders 'why so few visitors to Cornwall are attracted to these parts'.

The use of the moor by the holiday-maker on a sizeable scale is a new portent and its implications will be considered in a later chapter. As we have seen, a number of moorland farmers are now supplementing their income by the provision of camping sites and farm-house accommodation, but the majority of the visitors who make use of these facilities are not attracted by the moor itself. They come to the area because accommodation is cheaper there than it is in the coastal resorts or because, when the holiday season is at its peak, the seaside towns are full. It would be true to say that most of the visitors who occupy camp sites or rooms in the moorland area make their way to the beaches on every fine day. Nevertheless, the moor is no longer the remote and unknown region described by topographical writers in the early years of this century. Pony-trekking is becoming an increasingly popular form of exercise and motorists explore the byways on the moor in increasing numbers. A fine summer day brings scores of cars to park on Goonzion, Redhill Downs or Manor Common, and the wide view from Tokenbury Corner above Pensilva enjoys an exalted reputation. This is most evident at weekend and the majority of the cars carry West Country number plates. It would seem that Bodmin Moor, particularly the southern part of it, is much favoured by Cornish or Plymouth people who tend to avoid the coast in the high holiday season.

The popularity of the moor with local residents is also

demonstrated by surveys carried out by the Cornwall River Authority in 1970 and 1971 into the use of Siblyback Reservoir for fishing. In the first of those years 60.5 per cent of the anglers were local people and in the following year the percentage had risen to 77.8 per cent.

The moor falls within the territory of the North Cornwall and East Cornwall foxhounds and the Bolventor Harriers. In the final chapter of *The Bodmin Moors* by J. W. Malim (1936) there is an enthusiastic account of fox-hunting on the moor of which 'it has been declared by a competent authority that there is no better galloping country in England than is found here'. This again is an activity for local people and so to a considerable extent is the very different kind of sport, rock-climbing, which is confined to the eastern parts of the moor. There are short pitches on Hawk's Tor, and the Cheesewring quarry has been used by climbers throughout the present century. Though available to visitors by special permission the quarry is chiefly used by a Cornish grammar school. It is clear that the recreational use of Bodmin Moor is largely confined to local residents, although the visitor to Cornwall is becoming increasingly aware of its possibilities.

6   THE VILLAGES

A N Englishwoman of my acquaintance who is married to
a Welshman has propounded an interesting theory
based on her knowledge of the Celtic character. In her
view the Britons were not conquered by the Saxons, they
defeated themselves. It was their practice, she maintains, to
occupy an area until the squalor they had created was too
much even for them, whereupon they retreated, rather as the
Mad Hatter did at his tea-party, to make a fresh start. The
process was gradual but continuous and now the Celts stand
all along the western seaboard and push their rubbish over the
cliff. Certainly, untidiness is endemic to all Celtic countries,
including Cornwall, and when we add to this racial characteristic the intractable nature of granite as a building material, the
Celtic gift for improvisation, and the Cornishman's inde-
pendence and individualism, we can see that it was almost inevitable that the villages should lack grace and charm. And
the long-established tradition of the extractive industries has
played its part in rendering the Cornishman careless of, and
indifferent to, his environment. He is used to living in a mess.

It is fortunate that to this wide generalisation there are many
exceptions, but the visitor to Cornwall cannot expect to find
the warmth and elegance of a Cotswold village in a row of
Cornish cottages, and the churches, delightful though many
of them are, lack the dignity and splendour of the great wool
churches of East Anglia. Besides, Cornwall is a country of small
hamlets rather than large villages. This is 'the Celtic under-
writing' as W. G. V. Balchin calls it. Settlement, particularly
of this agriculturally poor hill land, was piece-meal and, in

general, enclosure was a long-drawn-out process and not a late development.

The name Newton, or in its Cornish form, 'Trenewth' or 'Trenoweth', is common in the moorland parishes. Farms bearing this name are usually on high ground at some distance from the main settlement and are an indication of the fact that the occupation of upland country developed in stages. The farms pushed up the valleys. These outlying farms, like the others, would have a considerable area of enclosed land right from the start. The farm-houses, instead of being gathered together in Saxon fashion would be scattered, each on its own land. This is to be expected where a pastoral rather than an arable economy predominates. The farmer would live where he could keep his eye on his stock and enclosure was necessary to protect the hayfields from marauding cattle and also because, on the granite, the surface moorstone had to be taken off the fields and dumped somewhere, and the most practicable way of dealing with it was to build it up into hedges. This has been the practice right down from Bronze Age times.

The Saxon occupation of Cornwall led to the development of an open field economy in some parts of the county, particularly in the north and east and adjacent to the towns, but it does not seem to have had much effect on Bodmin Moor and the surrounding areas. Indeed, it is unlikely that there was much settlement of this region in Saxon times, for Cornwall was thinly populated then and there was little inducement to settle on the moor.

Another factor that helped to determine the pattern of small settlements was the influence of the Celtic church. The early Welsh and Irish missionaries kept themselves to themselves. They settled, usually, in some quiet and sheltered spot remote from the main centres of population. That is why so many Cornish towns lacked a church until the late Middle Ages. The mother church of Callington is at South Hill, of Camelford at Lanteglos, of Penzance at Madron, of Wadebridge at St Breock. Similarly, in the rural areas we find the parish churches remotely situated for the most part, surrounded by not more than half a dozen houses and the main centres of population are elsewhere. Braddock, St Pinnock, Linkinhorne, Laneast, St Clether and Michaelstow are obvious examples. But some of the 'churchtowns' that surround the moor are quite sizeable places because they stand close to the moor's edge and settlement on the high land beyond them was necessarily sporadic and small in scale. We find, therefore, that St Cleer, St Neot, and Blisland are comparatively large settlements. Each is the metropolis of the area over which it presides.

On the moor itself there are only two settlements which are the centres of parishes, Bolventor, whose parish was a nineteenth-century creation and Temple which is a special case. Outside these two small areas, the moor is carved up between a number of ecclesiastical parishes, Advent, Davidstow, Altarnun, North Hill, Linkinhorne, St Cleer, St Neot, Warleggan, Cardinham, Blisland and St Breward. Three of these parishes, Altarnun, St Neot and St Cleer, in that order, are the largest parishes in the county and St Breward, Cardinham and Linkinhorne are all included in the first ten. Most of their churchtowns are snugly situated just off the edge of the moor and amongst them are some of the most charming villages in Cornwall.

In a description of these settlements one might begin with Camelford though it is not a churchtown, nor, indeed, is it a village. It was granted a charter as far back as 1259 and it had two members of parliament, and everything handsome about it. But it has never won much praise. Carew obviously had a poor opinion of it, for he says, 'Camelford, a market and fair (but not fair) town . . . yet steppeth little before the meanest sort of boroughs, for store of inhabitants or the inhabitants' store', Leland dubs it 'that poore village' and Celia Fiennes mentions its 'very indifferent accommodations'. So it goes on down through the centuries—'an inconsiderable place, none can possibly be more dismal'—'a dreary town'—'a dull little place without a vestige of nobility or suggestion of romance'.

Things have not been easy for Camelford. At one time it lay on the only main road through Cornwall, but in 1769 this was superseded by the direct route across the moor through Five Lanes and Temple. Just over 100 years later the railway came, but once again the little town was passed over. The surveyors had their eye on the Delabole slate quarry and the growing popularity of Boscastle and Tintagel, and there was also the need to cling to the 750ft contour. So the line went by more than a mile to the north of the town and though a station was built on a windy hill and euphemistically called Camelford, it did little to improve the town's status. Camelford tried to acquire the aura of Arthurian romance by making a modest bid to identify itself with 'many-towered Camelot' but did so without much confidence. For more than four centuries it did not even have a church of its own. The chapel of ease, dedicated to St Thomas the Martyr and founded in 1311, was desecrated under the 1545 Act and became ruinous. In 1786 the December issue of the *Gentleman's Magazine* reported,

> The ruined walls of Camelford chapel remained in the memory of people now living. The owner of the Bell Inn which is opposite, having for several years kept his stacks of furze therein and he falling into distress, was obliged to sell the inn to a neighbouring gentleman of large fortune, who seized on the chapel as an appurtenance to the inn, and leased out the spot for building an alehouse to which it hath been almost ever since applied.

Camelford had to wait until 1950 for its church to be rebuilt. The attractive little building adds much to the charm of the town centre which, in spite of what the topographers have said, is delightful. The wide street at the bottom of the town with the new church and the tiny park with the river running at its foot is unpretentiously satisfying and the scene is given a focal point by the early nineteenth-century town hall, a well proportioned building crowned by a camel instead of a weather-cock. Camelford, of course, derives its name, not from the quadruped but from 'Cam-alan' (crooked river), the old name for the

Camel. It is the river that lends so much charm to the place. Narrow openings between the houses give glimpses of it and provide access to an attractive riverside walk down to Pencarrow.

When *Cornwall, Coast Moors and Valleys* was published in 1930 on behalf of the CPRE, a Camelford filling station was selected to adorn the rogues' gallery of disfigurements which appeared in the book. The little town has moved a long way since then. Certainly, of its town centre it could be said that all recent changes are changes for the better. Most of the latest development has taken place at the top of the town, away from the main street and the older part of the settlement has been very little changed.

Lanteglos, the parish church, must not be confused with the church of Lanteglos-by-Fowey and there would be no possibility of confusion if the ancient name, 'Nanteglos' (the valley church) had been retained. It suffered the usual despoliation at the hands of the Victorian restorer. There are remains of the original cruciform Norman building, but the aisle and tower were added in the fifteenth century. In the churchyard is a pillar with an Anglo-Saxon inscription. The chief interest the church has is its beautiful and secluded position. It stands in the valley of the Laine, a tributary of the Camel. There are only a few houses including the large rectory, now an hotel. In the rectory garden are a number of gravestones, memorials of household pets which were set up by a late Victorian rector, a great animal-lover, of whom it is remembered that he once married two of his spaniels in church. He was a well-to-do bachelor given to hospitality. There were three great annual dinner parties and his invitations to these revealed a nice discrimination and a careful evaluation of the social status of his guests. This resulted in a good deal of heart-burning, for though the local society was a very stable one, some promotion or relegation from one division to another was inevitable from time to time. His other claim to fame is that he owned a walking stick for every day in the year.

On the summit of the hill between Camelford and its parish church is the curiously named hamlet of Valley Truckle. The name is, however, a corruption of the Cornish 'Velyn-Druckya', or tucking mill. In 1569 there was a fulling mill in the valley below and a house nearby still bears the name of Tuckingmill. The *West Briton* newspaper in a report on the annual meeting of the Cornwall Agricultural Society at Bodmin in 1811, says that it featured an exhibition of specimens of cloth manufactured at Camelford from the wool of merino sheep.

There are records of an indulgence granted by Bishop Vesey in 1521 in favour of Camelford Bridge. The present town bridge, however, is only about 100 years old. A little to the north of it a lane turns in to the hamlet turned suburb of Tregoodwell, and makes its way to Roughtor Ford. The moor rises less than a mile to the east of the town and one is always conscious of it. Camelford, which shares Bodmin Moor's heavy rainfall, is essentially a moorland town.

North of Camelford the main road rises to close on 1,000ft into the bleak lonely parish of Davidstow. Its air of desolation has become more marked in recent years since the aerodrome constructed there during the war was abandoned. There is no village of Davidstow, only a few houses and the church beside the main road to Launceston. The interior of the fifteenth-century church was completely transformed in 1875, but there are a few ancient benchends in the south aisle. During the eighteenth century the parish suffered from a succession of non-resident parsons. One can hardly be surprised at the unwillingness of the Georgian clergy to live in Davidstow, for though it stood beside the principal road into the county, it must indeed have been an isolated place.

Very different is Altarnun, or Altarnon as it should properly be called, for it takes its name from the patron saint, St Nonna, the mother of St David of Wales whose church we have just left. Most of the parish is open moorland, but the village is a snug secluded place tucked into the sheltered valley of the Penpont Water. The finely placed church is chiefly remarkable for its

Norman font and its wealth of ancient woodwork. Robert Daye, a local craftsman of the early sixteenth century, was responsible for the benchends of which seventy-nine remain. The rood screen which occupies the full width of the church is ancient too as are the communion rails which run from wall to wall. In the sanctuary are two Elizabethan paintings. One of them depicts the celebration of the Eucharist with the priest standing in a westward-facing position beyond the altar. Until these days of liturgical reform the Pope of Rome and the Vicar of Altarnun were the only two clerics in all Christendom who customarily celebrated the Eucharist from the eastern side of the altar, facing the congregation.

One is surprised to learn that the church tower is 109ft high, only 14ft less than Probus, the tallest tower in Cornwall. Its loftiness is obscured by its sheltered position against a steep hillside and its backing of trees. The impression is one of peace and seclusion in contrast to the open windswept acres on Trewint Downs, Carne Downs and Hendra Beacon which stand over it. It seems a typical site for a Celtic monastery and it is probable that one existed there before the Conquest.

The church and parsonage stand by themselves to the west of the river and the village—Penpont is its name, not Altarnun —is on the other side of the water. Church and village are linked by a narrow and ancient bridge. 'No prettier picture can be found in Cornwall than Altarnun Bridge with the tall grey Church and swelling churchyard beyond it,' wrote Charles Henderson in 1928. He might have written less enthusiastically today for the bridge is inadequate for modern traffic, and the ford nearby has now been spanned by a somewhat unattractive concrete structure. But if you stand at the lower end of the village street and look westwards, it is not the modern bridge that catches the eye but the fine church in its noble setting. The view in the other direction is equally pleasing. You look up a street of handsome but unpretentious cottages, amongst which stands the Methodist church built at the end of the eighteenth century. Over the door is a head of John Wesley carved by Nevil Northey Burnard in 1836 when Burnard was eighteen years old. Burnard was a local boy who, through the generosity of Sir Charles Lemon, MP, was enabled to develop his natural gift for working stone by studying in London and he achieved a national reputation as a sculptor. His end was a sad one, for eventually, broken by the death of his daughter and reduced to poverty by drink, he returned to Cornwall and suffered a pauper's death in Redruth workhouse in 1878. He had great talents and this little village is justly proud of him. 'Here lived Burnard who with his finger's bone/Broke syllables of light from the moorstone,' wrote the Cornish poet Charles Causley.

From the Penpont Water you move up the well-kept village street to the hamlet of Five Lanes on the A30 trunk road. Here there is an ancient inn, formerly the London Inn and now known as The King's Head. This was described in 1797 as 'the best situated inn in Cornwall' and was a changing house for the mail coaches. Five Lanes is a focal point for farmers from miles around and a large market is held here weekly.

A quarter of a mile along the main road towards Bodmin is the hamlet of Trewint on the edge of the moor. To turn to the left, forsaking the hurtling traffic, is to go back 200 years in 20yd. A narrow street threads its way between traditional cottages, one of which is famous. It was the house of Digory and Elizabeth Isbell who entertained the early Methodist preachers as they passed through on their way to west Cornwall. The first of these visits is described by John Nelson in his journal of a Cornish preaching journey in 1743:

One day, having travelled twenty miles without baiting we came to a village and enquired for an inn, but the people told us there was none in the town, nor any on our road within twelve Cornish miles, then I said 'Come, brother Downes, we must live by faith.' When we had stood a while I said 'Let us go to yonder house, where the stone porch is, and ask for something,' so we did and the woman said, 'We have bread, butter and milk and good hay for your horse.' When we had refreshed ourselves I gave the woman a shilling, but she said she did not desire anything. I said 'I insist upon it.' We got to Bodmin that night, but it was late before Mr. Wesley and Mr. Shepherd arrived, having lost the path on the twelve-mile common, and found the way again by the sound of the bells.

Digory Isbell, on whose tombstone it was written that he 'strictly adhered to the Duties of the Established Church', was profoundly influenced by the early Methodist preachers. Inspired by the account in II, Kings, of the Shunamite woman and her husband who built a room onto their house for the use of the prophet Elisha, he extended his cottage by adding two small rooms, one up and one down, for the accommodation of the preachers as they journeyed through Cornwall. This was before the road across the moor was constructed, when the only route was a bridle path. Wesley tells us that in April 1744 he was conducted 'over the great moor' by Digory Isbell because a fall of snow had obscured the track. These early visitors would have been glad of a place of refuge at Trewint where they might refresh themselves before tackling what was sometimes a hazardous journey.

The cottage was bought by the Methodist Church in 1950, and it was restored and furnished in eighteenth-century style. The rooms built on by the Isbells are open to the public and contain an interesting collection of 'Wesleyana'.

South-east of the main road, just below the moor, are a number of attractive farmhouses, for this is the Trebartha estate, one of the Domesday manors. It was acquired by a Norman knight after the Conquest and held by his family until the end of the fifteenth century, when it passed from the Trebarthas to the Spoures by the marriage of Anna Trebartha, the heiress, to one of Henry VIII's captains who had been sent to Cornwall to quell the rebellion of 1497. The Spoures remained at Trebartha until 1729, when once again there was no male heir. Mary Spoure, the heiress, was betrothed to her cousin, Francis Rodd, but, dying before the marriage took place, she left it to him by will. The Rodds rebuilt Trebartha Hall soon after it passed into their hands and held the estate until 1940 when, for the first time since the Norman Conquest, the place was sold.

The hamlet of Trebartha is a tiny place which still seems to be very much under the shadow of the great house even though this no longer stands, for the mansion was demolished soon after World War II. A few attractive houses line the narrow road which borders the park wall. The road then turns sharply to the east and climbs to North Hill. If you turn before reaching the village you will see a wonderful view—the gracious parkland of Trebartha and the woods behind it going up the steep hillside to the open moor, with the crags of Hawk's Tor overlooking the gap down which the Witheybrook thunders. In the other direction the handsome clear-cut outline of the church tower stands out against the sky.

The church is reminiscent of St Neot. It has a battlemented south aisle and a two-storey porch with stone tunnel vaults of similar pattern. The waggon roofs of the two churches are also much the same. Sir Nikolaus Pevsner suggests that the masons who built St Neot moved on to North Hill and built the tower and south aisle immediately afterwards. St Neot is famous for its stained glass and North Hill for its magnificent monuments, particularly the Spoure monument of 1688, in which we see the realistically coloured kneeling figures of Henry Spoure and his wife with two children standing in niches behind them. 'One of the most endearing monuments in Cornwall', Pevsner calls it and it has a warmth and intimacy so often lacking in memorials of the dead. Nearby is a slate monument to the infant Richard Spoure who died in 1623 in his third month:

> This carved tombe The sad inscription bears
> Of my soone death, And of my Parents' tears.
> For my departure, Though that happy I
> By that was freed From future misery:
> And now instead of their Fond Dandling Kisses
> I now enjoy a heaven—A heaven of blisses.

There is another Spoure memorial, a slate panel against the

south wall of the Trebartha aisle which commemorates Henry Spoure who died in 1603.

At the other end of the church is an elaborate slate tomb chest of Thomas and Jane Vincent, dated 1606 and, at the east end of the south aisle, a fragment of slate on which is depicted a child wrapped in its chrisom. Children who died within a month of baptism were usually buried in the chrisom or christening robe. This fragment was formerly in the chapel at Trebartha Hall and described as far back as 1694 as 'a very ancient Tombe'. This collection of monuments, remarkable anywhere, seem particularly impressive in this remote and beautiful place. They are human documents speaking out of the past with a clear and commanding voice.

The village, unlike most Cornish settlements, huddles in to the south side of the church. It is a collection of oldish houses, many of them slate-hung, clustered together along two narrow, twisty streets. From the churchyard wall one looks down immediately into a farmyard and there is another farm-house in the street only 30yd away. It is a quiet unspoilt place on the eastern slope of the Lynher valley facing the loveliest part of Bodmin Moor.

Beyond North Hill the perimeter of the moor reveals much evidence of its vigorous industrial past. Just over 100 years ago the copper mines of the Caradon district were the most important in the world and the area is thickly covered with settlements, most of which came into being in the mining days. They were, quite literally, mushroom villages, for they sprang up overnight. Two-roomed shacks were hastily built by the miners themselves on waste land at Minions, Pensilva, Crow's Nest, Darite, Tremar and Commonmoor. These miserable shanties have long since disappeared, but all the villages in the uplands of the parishes of Linkinhorne and St Cleer still have a fair proportion of Victorian cottages, the relics of the days of the mining boom. Most of these villages have had a recent face-lift and some of them, particularly Pensilva where the builders have been cashing in on the panoramic views it offers, have grown in recent years. The most attractive and unspoilt of these settlements is Henwood, which stands on a steep slope below the top of the pass where the narrow lane from King-beare goes over between Langstone Downs and Notter Tor. The conical Sharp Tor overhangs it as Mount Sinai overhung the village of Morality in *The Pilgrim's Progress*. The road from Henwood across the shoulder of Stowe's Hill opens up wide views with Callington and Kit Hill in the middle distance and the rampart of Dartmoor beyond.

At the top of the road one comes to Minions. The name suggests pampered darlings but there is nothing namby-pamby about this place. It is the highest settlement in Cornwall, standing at 1,000ft and surrounded not only by the stone circles and barrows of the distant past, but also by the relics of the nineteenth-century mining industry. In spite of its high position it is not particularly exposed. A short walk across the moor reveals how cunningly it is sited in a slight dip, well protected from the prevailing wind. In rough weather one can generally find cattle and ponies in its winding street. A hundred years ago it stood at the centre of great industrial activity. West Phoenix, Phoenix United, East Phoenix, Wheal Jenkin, Marke Valley, Gonamena, Craddock Moor—all these mines stood within a mile of Minions; the Liskeard–Caradon railway passed within a couple of hundred yards of the attractive cottages that still stand and remind us of what a small Cornish industrial settlement was like in the last century.

Tremar, where the houses are well set back from the road, is another attractive place. So is Commonmoor in its cul-de-sac north of the Minions–Redgate road, but these two settlements, like Pensilva, are fast becoming simply Victorian nuclei of rapidly increasing bungalow development. These old mining villages are not ghost towns, they have not withered and decayed like the mine buildings where their original occupants went to work, and this is to be commended. At the same time the urbanising of this wild corner of Cornwall has an un-planned appearance that causes some misgivings.

This new urban sprawl can be seen very clearly from the hill on which the village of St Cleer stands. This is an ancient settlement which as Carew tells us, 'brooketh his name by a more piercing than profitable air, which in these open wastes scoureth away thrift as well as sickness'. The wastes are no longer open, for the houses stretch all the way down the road past the holy well to Tremar; there is considerable development beside the lane to Rosecraddock and if you stand on the north-facing slope on which the church is situated and face towards Craddock Moor and Caradon, you look over an area in which there has been steady building development since the early 1960s. From the main street the church, in its tree-fringed churchyard, has an air of being in a sheltered and secluded position, but its noble tower is a prominent landmark for miles around. There was a small Norman church on the site but only two fragments of this early building remain, the Norman doorway, which is now inserted in the north wall and the bowl of the font. The north aisle was added in the fourteenth century and in the fifteenth, the great age of Cornish church-building, the church was largely rebuilt and the 97ft tower added.

If you go up southwards by a footpath between the houses that line the street facing the church, you emerge onto St Cleer Common, crowned by granite boulders and bordered by some attractive houses. From its summit you have one of the widest views in south-east Cornwall, across to Dartmoor and down to the estuary of the Tamar. Northwards you see the line of the moor, Caradon and the sweep of Craddock Moor with the ruined engine-houses on the skyline. You realise that St Cleer is essentially a moorland village, enclosed as it is by wild country on both sides. This large and expanding place is a good centre from which to visit the interesting collection of antiquities that belong to the parish, the Hurlers, Trethevy Quoit, the holy well and King Doniert's Stone.

Westwards from St Cleer village the land slopes down to the valley of the Fowey and beyond that is the parish of St Neot, the subject of the next chapter of this book. Beyond that is

Warleggan, a narrow wedge of a parish that reaches up into the hills between the much larger areas of St Neot and Cardinham. Until recent years this was the most remote place in Cornwall, for the only road that reached it came to an end on open moor at Calloways Water, a mile beyond the village. Now the lane has been extended to meet the moor road that links the A30 with the A38. The preliminary work on this half-mile of road across Redhill Downs was done by the local farmers on a voluntary basis. It now provides easy access for Warleggan people to Five Lanes and Launceston.

The main settlement in this small parish is the roadside hamlet at Mount which bestrides the old main road from Liskeard to Bodmin. To the south of it stood the Elizabethan house of Trengoffe (the house of the smith), beautifully photographed in Betjeman's *Shell Guide to Cornwall*. Now it is a ruin, having been gutted by fire in the late 1960s.

The churchtown, a minute place, is reached from Mount by a hilly and twisty road which turns away at the corner of Treslea Downs and runs steeply down into the wooded gorge of the Bedalder. Beyond Wooda Bridge the lane narrows and goes up between high banks to the village above. The sense of seclusion is very strong, but from the village street there is a charming view of the Bedalder valley and Panters Bridge below. From the bridge two rough and precipitous lanes lead up to church and village. These were Warleggan's only link with civilisation before the road from Mount was made.

The church stands above the village and away from it, half hidden in trees. It was one of the few Cornish churches that carried a spire, but this was destroyed by lightning in 1818 and has not been replaced. The building has thirteenth-century features but most of it, as usual, belongs to the fifteenth century. Before it was linked with a neighbouring parish Warleggan seems to have specialised in rather odd incumbents. Within living memory the parson here was an eccentric whose activities are vividly described in Daphne du Maurier's *Vanishing Cornwall* and are still remembered by many people in the locality. A friend of mine once attended Evensong at Warleggan Church and found herself the only member of the congregation. She had mistaken the time of service, arrived late and found the vicar in full career preaching eloquently to an empty church. Looking back over 500 years you find another eccentric incumbent. This was Ralph de Tremur who was instituted in 1331 but, with the bishop's permission, he was non-resident so that he might study at Oxford. He developed pronounced heretical views and twenty years later he travelled around Devon and Cornwall spreading his doctrines. He was said to have been able to speak fluently in Latin, French, English, Cornish and Breton, and was something of an intellectual snob. It is also recorded that he stole a pyx and committed the Host to the flames. He never resided at Warleggan, but after he had resigned the living he visited the parish, robbed his successor of his goods and set the parsonage on fire.

The churchtown of Cardinham is also a tiny place, for this beautiful parish follows the normal Celtic pattern, with small hamlets at Fletcher's Bridge and Millpool and a scatter of houses snugly situated in its deep and wooded valleys. The church is a noble building which has not suffered as grievously as most Cornish churches from its nineteenth-century restoration. It contains some good benchends and, a rarity in Cornwall where slate is the usual material for memorials, a fine fifteenth-century brass to a former rector, adorned with the naïve inscription in dog Latin: *Hic iacet Thomas Awmarle Rector ecclesie de Cardynam. Rogo vos fratres orate pro me et ego pro vobis in quantum possum.* ('I ask you, brothers, to pray for me and I will pray for you as much as I can.') The brass is tucked away in the south-east corner of the sanctuary beside the high altar. The interesting crosses and inscribed stones in this parish have been considered earlier.

The holy well is at Trenance, half a mile to the north of the church. Thomas Quiller Couch says that 'according to tradition' there was a chapel nearby and his daughters, Mabel and Lilian Quiller-Couch, in their book on the holy wells of Cornwall state that the chapel was destroyed and its stones used for building outhouses at the farm near by. The farmer, they inform us, concealed his 'sacrilegious booty' by turning the carved faces of the stones inward 'thus concealing their value and original service'. Cornwall has a long record of despoliation of its ancient monuments. The destructive process is usually carried out more blatantly. The holy well is still plainly visible.

Cardinham is at the south-west corner of the moor and the line of the hills which runs only a mile to the north of the church, does not exceed 900ft. Above the hamlet of Millpool between St Bellarmin's Tor and the Iron Age camp of Bury Castle is a rifle range, and movement on the wide and attractive Cardinham Moor is restricted when firing is in progress. The lower part of the parish contrasts sharply with these uplands. The pleasantly wooded country is carved up by the two headwaters of the Cardinham river which comes down from the moor to join the Fowey below the mansion of Glynn, built for Lord Vivian who was one of Wellington's generals.

The manor of Blisland, or Bliston, to give it its ancient name, was once crown land held by Harold Godwinsson, the last of the Saxon kings. Its village is one of the most beautiful places in Cornwall. It has a green, an unusual feature in this county where there are only sixteen village greens altogether, with a total area of only 10 acres. The Blisland green, rather more than an acre in extent, slopes gently down to the west and south. It is adorned with a collection of mature ash and elm trees and through the branches one can see the silver-grey of the ancient granite houses which flank the green to the north and west. The manor house, a noble building of great age and recently restored, is the largest and most impressive of these but all of them are attractive. The church, built into the hill-side on the lower side of the green, offers a surprise. As you enter it you look past the usual austerity of grey granite pillars at a riot of colour. The rood screen by F. C. Eden, set up in 1894, runs the full width of the church and is vividly painted. It conveys a strong impression of what most of our village churches

I

were like in pre-Reformation times. The church has something of all styles, from Norman to Perpendicular, and is of unusual design for the tower is built at the west end of the north transept. There are two fonts, the earlier, a circular one and recently discovered, is Norman work and the other is an octagonal font dating from the fifteenth century. There is an elegant seventeenth-century pulpit, carefully restored. On the north wall of the Lady Chapel is a somewhat crudely designed slate memorial tablet to Humfry Kempe who died in 1624. Under the figure of Kempe, his wife and his sons and daughters, some memorial verses are incised. In carving the penultimate line, 'Dyde? No, went hence, for they that leave posteritie—' the carver got himself into difficulties and the word 'that' is squeezed in above the rest of the line. One wonders what the Kempe family of Lavethan had to say about this when the job was completed. Mistakes of this kind are not uncommon. In St Neot churchyard is a gravestone on which the final e of 'tribute' is carved above the rest of the word as an afterthought.

By tradition the church bears the unusual dedication of SS Protus and Hyacynth but there is no written record of this. There was at one time a holy well in a field called Chapel Park some 300yd from the church. It was said of this field that if it were ever broken for tillage some frightful disaster would befall the family of the man who put it under the plough. In 1878 a crop of corn was grown in the field and at harvest time the farmer's son cut his knee so badly with the scythe that the leg had to be amputated. So the prophecy was fulfilled.

Blisland clings to the hillside above a pleasant stream which runs down to join the Camel at Merry Meeting. Its air of gentle seclusion is in sharp contrast to the hill country just above it. Pendrift, a pleasant hamlet, less than a mile to the north-west has open moorland at its doors and the expanse of Trehudreth Down skirts the isolated farmhouses above the stream which passes through the village of Waterloo.

St Breward, the next parish to the north belongs to the hill country, and is a very different sort of place. It is really a collection of small hamlets strung out along the hillside above the Camel: Penpont, Row and, at the top of the ridge, Churchtown, with the weather-beaten church tower as its apex. The church is dedicated to St Bruerdus but in the sixteenth century the village was called Simonward and Tonkin tells us that, according to popular belief, Simon Ward was a domestic brewer to King Arthur! St Aubyn, who has much to answer for, gave the sadly decayed building a severe going-over in the mid-nineteenth century. There was a Norman cruciform church here before major alterations were made in the fifteenth century. Rowlandson used this church to illustrate 'Dr Syntax Preaching' in *Dr Syntax's Tour* published in 1812. His illustration shows the bewigged parson expounding the Word from his three-decker pulpit, the moribund parish clerk below and a large and mainly inattentive congregation spread around the church, which is recognisable in Rowlandson's cartoon in spite of the later restoration. Rowlandson used to stay in the nearby mansion of Hengar in St Tudy parish and did a number of paintings of the beautiful Camel valley.

South-west of the church are the remains of a holy well. It stands beside an ancient and overgrown trackway in the Camel valley about half a mile below St Breward school. It looks today much as it did when Thomas Quiller Couch sketched it more than 100 years ago.

Behind the village, the open moor comes right down to the houses. Although there are numerous areas of enclosed land you can make your way from St Breward to the other side of the trunk road, five miles away, without crossing a hedge. Just below the church is the beginning of the road which cuts across the corner of the moor to Blisland and a few yards along it a lane turns off and leads up into the hills. The signpost used to direct one romantically and vaguely to 'the moor'. Now it is more explicit and points to 'Case Hill and the Candras'. This detailed direction will bring you eventually to three houses which stand beside a stream that comes down from Candra Hill to the Delank. They are served now by a well-surfaced road equipped with passing places as it runs over the open moor on the shoulder of Alex Tor. Until recently the only access was a rough cart track, the ancient road which went on past King Arthur's Hall to Garrow Tor. As you look back from the ridge, St Breward's Church is below you and looking sheltered enough in its belt of trees, but from the west it is an isolated and prominent landmark all the way to the coast, standing sentinel above the sprawl of the village it serves.

The road that passes the church climbs to the ridge above the Camel and offers one of the finest views in Cornwall. To the east are the bold outlines of Roughtor and Brown Willy and the rounded summit of Alex Tor, all in the parish. To the west across the wooded valley of the Camel is Hellesbury or Michaelstow Beacon with the Iron Age camp and ruined chapel at the top. Beyond is the long coastal ridge stretching from Delabole, past the tower of St Endellion, to the Camel estuary, with Stepper Point and Trevose Head in the distance. Southwards you see the array of pyramids of china-clay waste on Hensbarrow. A moorland walk along the ridge over Wood Park, past the Domesday manor of Hamatethy and across the gorge of the Henon river will take you to Advent. There is no village here, only 'a sad little church' as Betjeman calls it, standing in a field.

Bolventor is a small hamlet standing at 800ft on a bleak hilltop in the centre of the moor. It owes its existence to the road made over the moor as a result of a Turnpike Act of 1769. Before that date it was only a bridle path, though an attempt to popularise the route and render it more convenient for travellers was made in 1742 when posts were set up to mark it at quarter-mile intervals (but as we have already seen the early Methodist preachers had some difficulty in finding their way from Trewint to Bodmin). The famous Jamaica Inn was a changing house for coaches. On the route between Truro and Launceston horses were changed at approximately seven-mile intervals at Ladock, Indian Queens, Roche, Bodmin, Bolventor and Five Lanes. A bill naming the inn and dated 1789 is still extant. The 1859 edition of Murray's *Handbook for Travellers* states, 'this inn is frequented by sportsmen in the winter and affords comfortable though somewhat rude accommodation' and a newspaper advertisement of 1858 describes the inn as accommodating hunting parties. Now its high season is the summer, not the winter, and it does a brisk trade with the holiday visitor, not only because it is the only licensed house between Five Lanes and Bodmin, but because of the publicity it acquired from Daphne du Maurier's novel. Bolventor became a separate parish in 1846 when the church was built by Squire Rodd of Trebartha. It was provided to serve a growing community, for it was in that year that a good deal of undeveloped land in the area was disposed of by this landowner on ninety-nine-year leases. Many of the farmhouses around Bolventor and the fields that enclose them date from that time.

Temple is a deserted village, the only one I have ever seen. Some years ago not a single person lived in the township! (a curacy appendant to Blisland) and only one little farmhouse is now inhabited:—the ruins of half a dozen or more; the body of the church down; the chancel remains. Goldsmith, surely, must have travelled this road!

So wrote William Marshall in 1769. It must have been at about that time that the whole of the male population, which meant both of them, was hanged for sheep-stealing.

Temple's history began in the twelfth century when the Templars built a hospice there for the relief of travellers. In 1323 it passed to the Knights Hospitaller. From the Reformation it was outside the jurisdiction of the bishop and was a sort of Gretna Green, a centre for irregular marriages, until in 1774 it became subject to the normal diocesan discipline. It would seem that an early and determined effort was made to clean up the place, for Maclean quotes the case of Edith Gilpin of Temple in 1777. Having been presented at the Archdeacon's Court for having had a base child, and having submitted herself and confessed her crime, she was sentenced to perform penance. She was required on two succeeding Sundays, barefooted, bareheaded and wearing a white sheet, to make a public confession of her sin 'after the Second Lesson' at the morning service in the churches of Blisland and Cardinham. As Marshall states the church of Temple was ruinous at that time, this may account for the fact that it was the two neighbouring parish churches that had the benefit of her performance.

During the last years of the eighteenth and the greater part of the nineteenth century it seems that there were no religious services at Temple and the nominal care of the parish was in the hands of the incumbents of neighbouring parishes. The vicar of Liskeard, twelve miles away, had this responsibility at the end of the seventeenth century; in the 1760s it was the incumbent at Blisland; in 1840 it was the rector of Warleggan, in 1880 the vicar of St Neot and in 1882 the rector of Helland. In 1880 occasional services were held in the ruins of the church which was entirely rebuilt in 1883. Incorporated in the building that stands beside it are some ancient crosses that came from different parts of the parish and the piscina of the original church.

Temple lay on the original course of the turnpike and bridges, which still stand, were built over the two headwaters of the Bedalder which pass on either side of the hamlet. The main road now runs on the other side of Temple Tor. During the nineteenth century the population of this tiny parish varied between 37 and 12. Standing, as it does on the narrow loop road, the village remains a small and peaceful place.

There is one other settlement on the moor that deserves mention. This is Bradford, even smaller than Temple and in no way likely to afflict a Yorkshireman with nostalgia. Half a dozen houses cluster around a gorse-decked wastrel through which the Delank runs as it turns westward under Carbilly and goes down to Delphy Bridge. Here is almost everything that the lover of the moor requires, a dancing stream, a nicely proportioned clapper bridge, an avenue of trees and beyond, in contrast, a jumble of pocket-sized fields on the hillside, some of them well stripped of moorstone and showing a verdant green, others covered with boulders and gorse bushes, as wild and untamed as the open moor itself. Above are the great piles of waste stone from the abandoned quarry and the ruined sheds to remind us of Bradford's industrial past. Through the gap where the river comes down from Bedrawle is a distant view of Brown Willy's long ridge. This is one of the loveliest places on the moor.

7 ST NEOT: A MOORLAND PARISH

THERE are a number of ways into St Neot and all of
them are memorable. The stranger usually comes by the
valley road which leaves the A38 at Twowatersfoot and
runs beside the Loveny, crossing the river twice as it threads
the gorge between Polmenna and Carnglaze. The route is enclosed by steep hillsides, thickly wooded with the swift stream
below until, suddenly, the valley opens and you see the village
spread out against a background of bare moorland interspersed with trees. Another attractive route is the moorland
road which runs south from the A30 near Fourhole Cross,
through sweeps of open down and groups of fields, past Lord's
Waste and Mennaridden to the top of Goonzion Down from
which there is a fine view of the village in its superb setting.
An Anglo-Saxon homily for the Feast of St Neot says, 'He then
sought a waste place throughout all this land to live in; and by
God's providence found it in the west of this country ten miles
from Petrocs-stow, where it is called Neots-stoke and he there
built himself a dwelling in a very fair situation.' So, indeed, he
did; it is one of the most beautiful village sites in Cornwall.

But perhaps the most interesting approach is by the narrow
tortuous lane which enters the parish at Draynes Bridge and
runs westward at the moor's foot. Tolkien might well have been
thinking of this road when he wrote the opening chapters of
his *Lord of the Rings* trilogy, for this is 'hobbit country', homely
and comfortable, with steeply tilting fields and scattered homesteads, patches of woodland and glimpses of bare hills above.
The lane runs between the usual Cornish hedges, but here and
there the view widens and you see Berry Down towering into

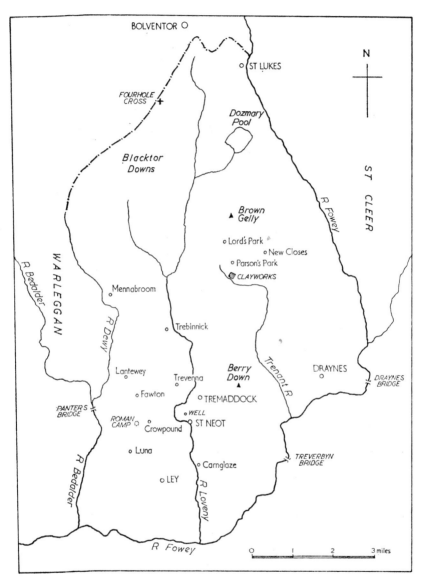

St Neot parish

the sky. The road climbs past Great Draynes farmhouse, drops
to the tiny hamlet of Draynes and rises again to the narrowest
part of its course. Over the brow of the hill a valley opens up, a
narrow ravine through the hills, but it looks spacious in contrast to the closely confined route you have been following. At
the bottom is the Trenant stream with a small chapel and
graveyard beside it, no longer used.

The road from Draynes Bridge joins the old coach road from
Liskeard to Bodmin at Wenmouth Cross. Three-quarters of a
mile beyond is the village which keeps itself concealed until the
very last moment. From Goonzion on the western side you see
the whole village spread out beneath you, but as you come in
from Trenant you see nothing of it until the church tower sur-
prises you through the trees. It seems a hidden, sheltered place.

At the time of the Conquest St Neot had a college of priests
but Count Robert of Mortain, who acquired the great manor
of Fawton, abolished the college, reserving only an endowment
of one priest. In 1095 his son, William, placed the church in the
hands of the Cluniac priory of Montacute in Somerset which he
had founded and the patronage rested with the priory until its
dissolution in 1539. Of the pre-Conquest church of St Neot
nothing remains but the cross-shaft in the churchyard of which
Henderson says, 'This is perhaps the finest ornamented cross in
Cornwall.' The shaft is decorated on all four sides with patterns
of interlaced work. In the late 1920s a portion of a cross-head
was found in the churchyard wall. It is a fragment of a wheel-
cross and is almost certainly a part of the cross-head of this
monument which must date from the ninth or tenth century.

The church was consecrated by Bishop Stapledon on 14
October, 1321 but of that building, too, little if anything
remains. The present church is mostly fifteenth-century work
and bosses on the roof of the west end of the nave bear the date
1480. The tower is earlier and the north aisle was rebuilt in the
second quarter of the sixteenth century.

The church is a fine and spacious place, although the general
effect is a little spoilt by the ornate screen erected at the begin-

ning of the present century. It stands higher than the original screen and is rather overpowering. The treatment of the east end of the sanctuary is not very satisfactory and the Ten Commandments which flank the high altar, and are now covered coyly with curtains, should suffer the fate of the original tablets of stone that Moses brought down from the Mount. Nevertheless, the general effect is elegant and dignified.

But visitors to St Neot do not come to look at the rood screen or the Ten Commandments, they come to inspect the windows. These are world famous and, with the possible exception of those at Fairford in Gloucestershire, the finest set of windows in any parish church in Britain. They were inserted in the late fifteenth and early sixteenth centuries and in twelve of the seventeen windows in the church more than half the glass is original. A major restoration was carried out between 1826 and 1829 by John Hedgeland who also designed four windows to replace the original glass that was too far gone for repair.

The finest of them all is the oldest, the Creation Window at the east end of the south aisle. This depicts the stories of the Creation, the Fall, the murder of Abel and the beginning of the story of the Flood which is continued in the Noah window which stands next to it. The Creation Window, the least restored of any, offers many delights: the newly created bird flying off the tip of God's finger, the smug self-satisfaction on Eve's face as she takes the apple and her grief-stricken expression as she is driven from Paradise; there is the naïve charm of Noah doffing his cap to his Creator. Two of the incidents are not derived from holy writ. There is the picture of the death of Cain, shot by an arrow from the bow of the blind Lamech. A sculptured representation of this can be seen on the west front of Wells cathedral. There is also a depiction of the death of Adam, a story familiar to the Cornish in medieval and early Renaissance times because it appears in the Cornish *Ordinalia*. This was written in the latter part of the fourteenth century at Glasney, where there was a community of secular canons, and describes how Seth journeys to the gates of Paradise, seeking the oil of mercy for his father, Adam. There is the tree of knowledge, now withered, but in its branches he sees a child. 'It was the son of God you beheld,' says the Cherubim, 'swaddled like an infant. When the time shall come, it is He who will redeem, equally with His body and blood your father Adam, your mother and all the righteous. He is the oil of mercy.' The Cherubim then bids Seth take three seeds from the apple that his father ate. 'When he dies, put the seeds without fail between his teeth and his tongue. In a short time you'll see that three trees have grown from them.' The window shows Seth placing the seeds in his father's mouth as he lies on a half-tester bed. In the background is the tree with the babe in the branches.

The lower half of the Noah Window has been considerably restored, but enough remains to reveal its original beauty. The representation of the ark is unusual. It is generally portrayed as a gabled shed resting in a barge, like the conventional nursery toy, but it is pictured here as a three-masted ship which might have borne Henry VIII to the Field of the Cloth of Gold.

It is probable that the original intention was to provide in these windows a conspectus of Old Testament history, but after the Creation and Noah Windows had been completed it would seem that funds ran short and it became necessary to encourage each of the well-to-do families of the parish to assume responsibility for a window of its own. The original scheme does not seem to have appealed to them. They wanted representations of their own patron saints and some of them had their own families represented in the lower lights of the windows. So in the Borlase Window we find Nicholas Borlase, his wife, Katharine, and their four sons and eight daughters. In the Martyn and Calway Windows the families of the donors are also depicted. When the supply of wealthy families ran out the parish had to revert to public subscription again and three of the windows in the north aisle were provided in this way, one by the wives of the western part of the parish, one by the young women and one by the young men.

Space does not permit a detailed consideration of these magnificent windows but mention should be made of the St George Window, now at the west end of the north aisle, though it was formerly on the south side. This is the only surviving church window in England which illustrates the legend of St George at length and it portrays his miraculous restoration to life by the Virgin Mary and, after the well-known dragon episode, his capture, suffering and martyrdom. The source of some of these incidents is not known. Most famous of all is the St Neot Window, the one presented by the young men of the parish. It contains representations of twelve incidents in the legendary life of the saint. Undoubtedly it is this window which has made Neot, as Canon Doble has said, 'of all the Cornish saints the one whose story is most familiar'. His extensive hagiography suggests that two persons have become confused. There is the Saxon saint honoured at St Neot's in Huntingdonshire, a man of royal blood associated with King Alfred, and there is also the Celtic Niet, or Anietus, around whom a number of fanciful legends have accumulated. We are told that his food was provided by an angel and that every morning he took for his daily needs one fish from the three which he found swimming in the holy well. One day his servant, Barius, decided to vary the saint's diet by bringing him two fishes, one boiled and one fried, but Neot ordered them to be returned to the water where they were miraculously restored to life. Another story describes how, when his oxen were stolen, a pair of stags came and offered their necks to the yoke. It is said that he rescued a doe from the hunters and that he was so small that he had to open his church door by throwing the key into the lock. Most of these legends in their charming simplicity are portrayed in the window. There is nothing like it anywhere else in the world.

There is a Latin life of St Neot, *Vita Sancti Neoti presbiteri et confessoris,* in the Bodleian Library in a collection of lives of saints completed in the twelfth century. This states that the body of the saint was removed to Huntingdonshire. We are told that the removal of the body was commanded by St Neot himself in a supernatural appearance. The men of the village, however, took a more practical view of the matter. They regarded it as a simple case of theft and sent an armed force to bring the relics back. But the supernatural again intervened and they found it impossible to raise the body and take it home to Cornwall. This story, even without the supernatural embroidery, is difficult to accept. The stealing of relics was common practice in the Middle Ages, but it is scarcely credible that they would have been conveyed for a distance of 270 miles; the monks of the priory beside the Ouse could have enhanced the prestige of their religious house more easily. The record of the removal of St Neot's body to Huntingdonshire is almost certainly a fabrication and the saint honoured there is, as Mark Twain said of the writer of the plays attributed to Shakespeare, 'another fellow of the same name'. Preserved in St Neot parish church is a splendid piece of doggerel painted on board which sets out some of the saint's history. It informs us that his father was a Saxon king and that he gained fame as a preacher at Oxford, but it is firmly against the tradition that his body was removed to St Neots in Huntingdonshire.

> Some say his bones were carried hence,
>   St Needs will have it so,
> Which claims the grace of Neot's tomb,
>   But hereto we say, No!

But whether the relics of the saint remain in Cornwall or lie elsewhere, they seem to have accomplished one very sizeable miracle. It is remarkable that the windows remained in a state of fair preservation up to the time of the Hedgeland restoration. As David Gilbert says in his introduction to the sumptuous volume, *A Description of the Splendid Decorations Recently Made to the Church of St Neot in Cornwall* by J. P. Hedgeland (1830):

ST NEOT: A MOORLAND PARISH

When the lofty pretensions of the Roman Pontiff, Indulgences and Transubstantiation, were found to be unauthorized by the holy scriptures, zeal, most properly excited against Catholic abuses, directed its greatest fury in destroying every visible symbol of their former existence. Works of art, obtruding themselves on the senses, became peculiarly subject to the fury of destruction. The most splendid buildings were rased to the ground—crosses overthrown—works of sculpture and of carving were dashed to pieces, and paintings were rendered invisible by the ready application of lime; while the gaudy colour exhibited by stained glass in windows provoked a still more extemporaneous and amusing mode of annihilation.

The remote and sequestered situation of St Neot's Church may have been its protection against early Reformers and later fanatical armies; and it is probable that persons in the immediate neighbourhood retained, long after their becoming Protestant, a deep respect for the object of their former veneration and for the hero of their infantine tales.

Behind the pomposity and the prejudice there is sense in this. But the survival of the windows is surprising. During the Civil War St Neot was often on the edge of stirring events. Braddock Down, where there was a sharp engagement in January 1643, is only five miles away and in the next year St Neot must have seen much going and coming of troops in the Lostwithiel campaign. At the end of July in that year the Earl of Essex led the Parliamentary forces to Bodmin by way of Horsebridge and Linkinhorne. It seems almost certain that some of his troops would have passed through St Neot. The Royalist army followed through Trecarrell and Liskeard, there was movement of scouting parties on Caradon Down and St Cleer and on 9 August a troop of the King's horse was headquartered at St Neot. How the windows escaped injury in this turbulent time is a mystery, for we have documentary evidence of the fact that the parsonage, which is less than 30yd from the Creation Window, was reduced almost to ruin during the Interregnum and in 1680, Thomas Philpe, the vicar instituted in 1660 after the King had enjoyed his own again, wrote plaintively of the condition when he came to it. He gives a dismal account of the apple trees, the burning of the rafters and other timber:

> ... both of the dwelling and outhouses, taking away the glass and the iron barrs of the windows so that all was in the high way to a total devastation and none of these spoylors found of ability to make the least satisfaction so that the incumbent was necessitated to betake himself forthwith to building it if he would have any house to put his head in.

One relic of the Civil War remaining in St Neot Church is its copy of the King Charles Letter, written by the King 'from his camp at Sudeley Castle the 10th September, 1643', to the inhabitants of Cornwall, 'to perpetuate to all time the memory of their merits, and of our acceptance of the same'. Many Cornish churches lost their copies in the orgy of Victorian restoration, but thirty-four retain them. Another relic of Royalist sympathies is the oak branch on the top of the church tower. This was renewed every year on Oak Apple Day, 29 May, and the custom is still kept up. If you stand outside the south porch you will see it peeping over the battlements.

On the north side of the sanctuary is a very beautiful canopied recess which is popularly supposed to have contained the shrine of St Neot, but is more likely to be an Easter sepulchre. Within it are traces of a mural painting. At the other end of the church is a fine early seventeenth-century slate tomb-chest on which the kneeling figures of William Bere and his wife are carved in bold relief. Beneath the Latin inscription with its grim reminder, *Sum quod eris* ('I am what you will be') is carved a very competent piece of rhyming verse. It begins, as is typical of the period, with the punning phase 'Here lieth Bere whom Angells to heaven beare', and then eulogises the deceased: 'Faithfull he was to friends, skillful in lawe of man, Practis'd in law of god . . .' Then, after reminding the reader of the certainty of death, it concludes on a happier note: 'So when thou diest thy death no death shall be/ But passage unto life, the god of lyfe to see.'

This William Bere bought the manor of Trenay Fawton from the Tubbe family, donors of one of the windows in the church. William's daughter and heiress, Grace Bere, married Sir John Grylls of Lanreath who died in 1649. The marriage started the association of the Grylls family with St Neot. They have been great benefactors of the church and are still patrons of the living.

The list of incumbents is practically complete from 1266. In 1313 Bishop Stapleton appointed a coadjutor or guardian for the vicar, Sir Philip, who had contracted leprosy. The leper was confined to certain rooms in the parsonage and the coadjutor, Sir Ralph de Retyn, was ordered to pay him a yearly allowance for clothes and to provide him with food and drink. Robert Tubbe of the Trenay Fawton family, was vicar from 1508 to 1544. He seems to have been a man of considerable drive and organising ability, for it must have been he who was chiefly responsible for the provision of the church windows. Richard Bennett who succeeded him in the living was also vicar of St Veep where he lived in concubinage with Jane Earle who died in his house 'and was secretly buried in the night time within the parish church . . . whose death was not known unto the parishioners by the space of three years'. A charge of murder was brought against him at the inquest but it would not stick. He seems to have been an unsavoury and well-hated character for he was relentlessly pursued in this matter and was tried for murder at Launceston Assizes. The charge was found not proven. And although the inquest on Jane Earle was reopened and he was found guilty of her murder, the verdict was again made void for insufficiency. But he was hanged in the end for his part in the Prayer Book Rebellion, martyr rather than murderer. The record of Joseph Maye, who was vicar of St Neot and St Austell at the time of the Civil War, is altogether more pleasant. At the end of the war he was ejected from both livings but when, in 1648, there was plague in St Austell and the vicar appointed in his place had forsaken his post of duty, Maye returned and fearlessly ministered to the stricken congregation until the plague ceased.

The holy well is in the valley of the Loveny about 300yd

from the church. It plays a prominent part in the story of the patron saint, for not only did it provide him with his daily supply of fish, it was also, as we are informed, the scene of his regular devotions. Each day he was accustomed to stand up to his neck in its waters reciting the whole of the Psalter. Perhaps this accounts for the belief that he was extremely short in stature for the well is very shallow. James Michell in his *Parochial History of St Neots*, published in 1833, says, 'That there was an arch of stone over it, with a large oak springing from the arch, and with doors to the entrance was remembered by some old inhabitants of the parish lately deceased . . . Weakly children used, within memory, to be brought even so distant as from Exeter, to be bathed in the water of the well, on the three first mornings in May.' The original well covering had disappeared before Michell's time. The present building, typical of the early Tractarianism of its period, was provided by the Reverend Henry Grylls in 1862. It is charmingly sited in the level river meadow, backed by a steep bank thickly covered with trees.

The village of St Neot is the only large settlement in the parish. There are small collections of houses at Ley, at Panters Bridge, at Draynes and Tremaddock, but the churchtown is larger than all of them put together. It stands almost on the dividing line between the lands 'of a good quality and well adapted for corn and pasturage' as Michell puts it and the 'immense wastes' in the north. The richly wooded valleys of the Bedalder, Loveny and Trenant stream have an atmosphere of south Cornwall about them, but to the north of the old coach road, once you have passed through the Tremaddock gorge, you are in hill country. Letter Moor and Penkestle Moor at 800ft, and Draynes Common at 900ft look down past a tangle of fields to the wooded country below. In the north of the parish there are considerable expanses of moorland with the rounded hill of Brown Gelly as the highest point in the area. The charm of the village owes more to its situation than to any architectural excellence. There are a number of unpretentious but attractive houses built of the local stone, and the church is magnificently positioned on a level platform of land above them. There has been some recent building development on the outskirts of the village, but it has not yet overlaid the ancient settlement as it has done at Dobwalls, Pensilva and St Cleer. Nevertheless, if the character of the village is to be retained, careful planning is becoming increasingly necessary.

The parish is largely bounded by rivers, the Fowey on the east and south, the Bedalder and Dewy on the west. There is no natural boundary in the north. At a perambulation of the parish in 1613 the boundaries were defined as follows:

> On the north side the bounds of the said parish beginneth from a tenement in Alternun called Dryworks, by the river of Foye which divideth the said parish of St Neots from the several parishes of Alternun, St Cleere, Liskeard, St Pinnock and Braddock, until it come to a place called Bedalder-foot where the river of Bedalder falleth into the river of Foye. From Bedalder-foot the bound leadeth by the said river of Bedalder which divideth the said parish of St Neots from the parish of Warleggan until it come to the head-ware in the river above Pontwer's Bridge; and from thence by a little lake that falleth into the said head-ware until it come to the head of Dewey Moor; from Dewey Moor-head the bound leadeth to the marsh which divideth between the said parish of St Neots and the parish of Temple, until it come to Temple Causeway; from Temple Causeway the bound leadeth by the way to Peverell's Cross, otherwise Shorter Cross; and from that cross unto a place called Leathern Bridge; and from thence, bounding in several places in the moor called by the names of Stannum Hill and Stannum Ball it leadeth unto a place called Deephatches; from thence the bound leadeth unto the said place in the river of Foye from whence the bounds and the limits first began.

Most of this is clear enough. Dryworks, Bedalder-foot, Pontwer's (Panters) Bridge, Dewey Moor and Temple Causeway can still be identified; Stannum Hill is Stanninghill, a farm-house a quarter of a mile to the north-west of the A30 and Stannum Ball probably refers to a 'bal' or mine-working nearby. Peverell's Cross stands beside the main road further to the west in Blisland parish and cannot be the monument referred to in the 1613 document unless, as Henderson suggests, it has been moved in the last 150 years. Leathern Bridge cannot now be identified. Michell says that 'the large stones on which the bridge or causeway were anciently placed' had disappeared by his time, overlaid by 'the accumulation of soil and sand from the tin stream works'. It would seem that in 1613 the boundary of St Neot parish was farther to the north than it is now, for the present northern boundary of the civil parish does not cross the trunk road. No doubt the centre of the moor was a sort of no man's land in former days and the parish boundaries somewhat indefinite.

It may be that the parish once coincided with the manor of Fawton which was established in Saxon times and which appeared in the Domesday Book as Fawitona, the most important Demesne manor of Count Robert of Mortain. It extended from the Fowey right up to Brown Willy. In 1149 parts of it were given to the church of St Stephen of Launceston and the Canons of Launceston also benefited from a gift of lands from the manor. This included Trebennuc (Trebinnick) a farm which still exists on the fringe of the moor in the northern part of the parish. In 1170 another gift to the Canons of Launceston was made by the Lord of Fawton and the deed of gift includes names that can still be identified: Hungerhill, Pinnock's Hill and Dozmary. The Canons established a farm called Newhouse-in-the-Moor in St Neot and this, perhaps, is New Closes, two miles north of the village. Nearby are two settlements known as Lord's Park and Parson's Park. It may be that one remained in lay hands and the other belonged to the Canons. Henderson tells us that the great manor of Fawton was split up before 1450 and that one of the manors was called Trenay-Fawton. In Henry VIII's time this was bought by John Tubbe of Trengoffe in Warleggan. As we have seen, from the Tubbes it passed to the Beres and from them to the Grylls.

The map shows that a number of farm-houses in the parish

stand on the site of former manor houses. There is Fawton itself, there is Luna where the enclosure in which the ancient manor house stood can still be seen, there is Treverbyn, there is Trevenna. There are no great houses in the parish now. If Parson Tubbe were alive today and occupying himself with the business of extracting money from his parishioners so that he might beautify his church with painted glass, he would have no wealthy landed families to turn to.

In 1841 the population of the parish was 1,515, twice as many people as there are now. Those were the days when the Loveny valley was busy with mining operations. A detailed history of these operations would prove complicated for mines were continually opening, closing and reopening with fresh capital under another name. There is Wheal Mary, for instance. This mine, which operated on both sides of the river, began life in the middle of the eighteenth century as Pouldiste Copper Mine. It closed in 1773 and reopened half a century later as Wheal Mary Consols. In the four years from 1826 to 1830 it sold 2,500 tons of copper ore at prices of from £7 to £9 a ton. After a gap of six years it had another short lease of life from 1836 until 1839. Three years later Wheal Sisters was opened just to the north of it and in seven years raised 3,000 tons of ore which realised £17,000. In 1849 Wheal Sisters and Wheal Mary Consols joined forces and, soon after, the northern part of Wheal Mary Consols reopened under the name of Wheal Caroline and the southern lode was developed under the name of Lampen Consols. From 1828 until 1851 the Wheal Mary group of mines produced over 11,000 tons of copper ore which realised just over £56,000 and in the decade beginning in 1854, they raised another 2,000 tons which brought in just under £14,000. After the 1860s production continued on a very small scale. In the present century a company was floated, small Cornish stamps were erected near Wheal Mary counthouse and the area was combed for tin, which was mostly found in the surface spoil heaps. The square chimney stack of the burning house, or calciner, still stands in the field west of the river, near Lampen farmhouse. The work was intermittent and success was variable, so that local cynics christened the undertaking 'Wheal Jerk' and, later still, 'Balscat'. The second nickname is derived from two Cornish dialect words, 'bal' which means mine and 'scat', meaning bankrupt, which explains the hoary Cornish joke about the familiar Harvest Festival hymn, 'We plough the fields and scat—'.

The Wheal Mary complex of mines lies south of the village. So does Wheal Leather, near Polmenna, and some other undertakings in the vicinity of Ley and Luna. North of the village was Wheal Robins, started in 1839, and Wheal Trevenna which opened in 1845, ran for two years and then closed, but reopened for a further two years in 1864. It was at this mine, as Hamilton Jenkin reports, that the machinery was constantly breaking down and men were employed mending it far into the night. Food and drink had to be brought from the village to keep them in good heart for, as one of them pointed out, 'You must fill the sack before he will stand'. It is interesting and perhaps significant that this quip enshrines an agricultural metaphor. St Neot is a farming parish and the mining that took place there intermittently through the nineteenth century was a small-scale affair. In spite of the lack of success at Wheal Trevenna in the forties and sixties, the mine opened again in 1887 under the name of Tregeagle Mine, but perhaps the curse laid on the notorious character after whom it was renamed extended to cover the mine as well. A good deal of money was invested in surface machinery but the cost was not recovered. Yet another attempt was made as recently as 1908, but this also proved unsuccessful. Further north, on the edge of the moor and on the west side of the river, was Hobbs Hill Mine. The east bank was not neglected either, Wheal Hammett was the name of these workings.

Goonzion Down, the stretch of moorland on the hill to the west of the village has several well defined mineral lodes. All over the surface are the mounds and depressions that mark early mine-workings and these have given rise to yet another

St Neot legend. The story goes that the saint told his people that Goonzion Down was so rich in mineral wealth that the man who discovered it would be able to have his horse shod with silver. In spite of repeated questioning Neot was loth to give detailed information, but at last he told his flock that on a certain night he would place a feather on the spot beneath which the treasure lay. Next morning the miners assembled with the tools of their trade and found the whole area plastered with feathers. Certainly the surface workings on Goonzion are ancient, and underground prospecting did not begin until the 1830s. In 1846 a mine called Wheal Friendship had rights all over Goonzion Downs. Two of the shafts, Whim Shaft and Roaring Shaft have only recently been filled in. At the time of writing, a field below Goonzion on the edge of the village is being prepared for building and the soil turned over by the bulldozers is nearly all mining waste.

Some grass-grown spoil-heaps, a ruined cottage or two, the old leats, now dry ditches bridged over here and there with granite slabs, a gravestone—the first you see as you enter the churchyard from the west—of a miner who lost his life as the result of an accident in Wheal Mary, are all that remain to commemorate more than a century of mining in this quiet valley. The lost hopes, the lost fortunes, the hunger and despair have gone down into the past and are as remote from us as the honeycomb of ancient workings beneath the fields; the lush growth in the sheltered Loveny valley has obliterated the industrial scene. But though good money was made by some people and, as we have seen, the Wheal Mary mines alone yielded a return of over £70,000, the nineteenth century must have been a hard time for many. Up and down the valley are tiny cottages which housed large families clinging precariously to life, always on the very edge of starvation. From one of them, within living memory, the bread-winner walked each day nine miles across the moor to work his shift at the Stannon claypit and nine miles back at the end of it.

There was slate-quarrying, too. At Carnglaze where the

valley narrows three-quarters of a mile below the village, two large caves have been cut into the hillside, one at a lower level than the other. Their floors are covered with closely packed shale, the detritus of the quarrying operations, but even as it is, parts of these enormous caverns go up to a height of more than 50ft above the present floor level. The upper cavern is approximately 100yd in length and the lower one, which can be reached from it by descending a steep bank of loose slate, is about three times as large. In the lower cavern are two pools of water, one of considerable size and about 30ft deep. Though the domestic supply of the nearby house is drawn from the larger of the two pools the water-level remains almost constant. These interesting underground quarries are now open to the public and are artificially lit. The floodlit waters of the larger pool have an unbelievable clarity. During World War II, when so many remote and unexpected places were used as depositories for our national treasures, the abandoned slate quarries of St Neot also played their part in the national effort; they were used as a cache for the spare supplies of naval rum!

Although, like most country districts, St Neot is now attracting a number of retired people from outside, the bulk of its population form an indigenous group. The names on the gravestones can be seen on the voters' list in the church porch. Some thirty of its inhabitants are employed at the rapidly growing china-clay workings at Parson's Park, a few find work in the forestry plantations at the lower end of the valley, and a handful commute to Bodmin, or Liskeard, or Plymouth. The bulk of them still work on the land in small farms mostly run by the farmers and their families without the help of hired labour. Tourism brings its fringe benefits; cottages are let, visitors are boarded, several farms are in the pony-trekking business, caravans are accommodated here and there. But at the time of writing the parish is still a working area, not a playground. This is true of the whole of the moorland region and no part of it is less affected by the holiday industry than St Neot. In Cornwall tourism still concentrates upon the incomparable coast and St Neot is further from the sea than almost any place in the county, for it is twelve miles from the south coast and eighteen from the north. St Neot lies off the beaten track and is very conscious of its individuality.

This was revealed in recent years in a rather striking way. In 1967 it was discovered that the church roof was heavily infested with death-watch beetle and the estimated cost of repair was £7,000. This was a serious commitment for a thinly populated area lacking in wealthy landowners. If the money was to be raised it had to be through the efforts of the general community. So the people got to work to stage a festival. During the last week in April, 1968, though the cows were milked twice a day as usual, virtually no other farm work was undertaken, for most of the parishioners were otherwise engaged. There was a Festival of Flowers in the church, a dance in a local barn with a barbecue outside. A play was written for the occasion by a local resident and performed in the parish church. Nearly a hundred parishioners with an age range that extended from five to eighty careered around the narrow lanes in coaches, supplied free of charge by a neighbouring 'bus proprietor, who had not forgotten that he, too, had been born in the parish, and tramped the moorland to view the local antiquities. The children organised several yards of pennies in the village street and the church treasurer exercised his charm to make their parents get their cheque books out. Anglicans, Methodists and unbelievers all took part in a quite incredible display of unanimity to save their parish church from disaster.

Co-operation does not come naturally to the Cornishman. In spite of his motto, 'One and All', in spite of his national anthem with its reference to the 30,000 Cornishmen combining to rescue Bishop Trelawney, he tends to go his own way. But the St Neot Week of 1968 gave the lie to all that. To the parishioners themselves this was a glorious as well as a gregarious occasion. And profitable, too. When they had counted it all up they found that the Restoration Fund had benefited by more than £3,000.

It was not enough, of course, but the attack on the death-watch beetle started at once. The flowers went out and the scaffolding came in; the money was spent and an overdraft negotiated. In the meantime the parish prepared for another Week. This was staged two years later, in the summer of 1970. There was another topical play in the church and also a performance by the village primary school of a medieval pastiche on the St Neot legend in front of the holy well, with the audience seated around on straw bales (subsequently donated to the auction sale which took place towards the end of the week). Well-trained sheep and less well-trained sheep dogs went through their routine in the meadow below the church; the pony-trekkers lent their horses for a field day on the moors; there was a sponsored walk, a dog show, a gymkhana and other delights. By the end of the week close on £4,000 had been added to the funds. Donations and some other money-raising efforts produced a further £3,000, so that in one way and another this moorland parish had extracted the sum of £10,000 from its own members and the general public in just over three years.

This is a chronicle of very small beer but it provides evidence of the vitality and strong sense of community that can exist in a small rural area. Some of those who supported their church so wholeheartedly are unlikely to visit it again until they do so in a horizontal position, but in these two village festivals they backed their parish church, not only through naïve enthusiasm for an entirely new experience, but because it was the church of their parish.

The same spirit of local patriotism was manifested in a beating-of-the-bounds which took place in the autumn of 1971. The twenty-eight-mile circuit was accomplished on three successive Saturday afternoons by a group of parishioners of whom the youngest was under school age and the oldest nearer seventy than sixty. The limits of the civil parish are marked by a number of boundary stones and not long after this perambulation one of these stones was restored to its proper place by

Draynes Bridge. If the local historian, Michell, were living today he could not complain as he did in 1833 of his inability 'to induce the inhabitants of St Neot to renew the perambulation of their parish'.

The moors of St Neot are no longer 'a wide howling wilderness' as Michell describes them. Though a number of open areas remain, the stretches of unenclosed down are interspersed with human settlements and their adjacent fields, some of which, like Mennabroom, are of early date. The entrance gates of these scattered farmsteads in the hill country open onto motorable roads, but many of them lie well back from the public highway, surrounded by their own enclosed lands. Some still have no access except over rough tracks. Many of the moorland farm-houses stand on high and exposed sites unlike those at the lower end of the parish. Here the houses turn their backs to the downs and some, like Fawton and Hole and Lantewey are built into the hillside. There is no parish in Cornwall which reveals sharper contrasts. The lower, thickly wooded reaches of the river valleys are in a different world from the high marshlands between the rolling downs from which the rivers come. There, in the middle of the parish, at the point where St Neot set up his cell, is the village in its green crescent of meadow land. He must have had a good eye for country to settle there.

8 THE FUTURE OF THE MOOR

EVER since the day when Mesolithic man knapped his flint flakes on the shores of Dozmary Pool, the moor has proved itself able to survive everything that man has done to it. The stone circles, the hut settlements, the hill forts, the spoil heaps of mining waste are all reconciled to the natural environment. The gashes in the hillsides left by the quarrier now seem to be an integral part of the moorland scene and the ruined engine-houses around Caradon are evocative of a past which seems to have all the romance and none of the squalor of the industrial past. Its venerability and its chequered history of rapidly fluctuating fortunes both combine to invest the physical remains of the industry with an atmosphere which differs little in kind from the atmosphere of the Iron Age camp on Stowe's Hill.

But it would be unwise to assume that the marks of man's intervention will continue to be as easily absorbed as they were in the past. We live in an age when the pressures on the waste spaces of our overcrowded island are immense. The urgent needs of our economy, the inflated value of land and the heavy demands of organised tourism all threaten areas which in former times enjoyed immunity. The Lake District, the moors of the Pennines which border the great industrial centres, Snowdonia, the New Forest, Dartmoor are all under threat and a tiny area like Bodmin Moor is particularly vulnerable. The scale and scope of modern technology are such that great transformations are easily and quickly brought about and it is possible for the developments of a mere decade to change the character of an area for hundreds of years.

THE FUTURE OF THE MOOR

Every wild and open space in Britain is a vacuum which outside interests desire to fill. The industrialist seeks to exploit its natural resources, the house speculator, hungry for building land, clamours for entrance, the holiday-maker is looking desperately for elbow room. The eighty square miles of Bodmin Moor, almost the most westerly of the relatively undeveloped areas in England are under siege.

There is still a vast quantity of mineral wealth locked up in the metamorphic aureole and this has only been preserved because of the high cost of extracting it. Advances in mining techniques will soon make it possible for these assets to be exploited. The china-clay industry, though at present limited to only two areas in the moor, Stannon and Parson's Park, is vigorous, rewarding and expanding. It takes up a lot of room and it makes a good deal of mess. The abandoned clay-workings in various places on the moor, particularly in the Bedalder valley between Temple and Warleggan, show that this activity leaves its mark on the countryside for many years and the rapidly advancing lagoons of micaceous waste under Roughtor, and on the southern slopes of Brown Gelly, will insult the environment for a long time to come.

Agricultural development, too, is likely to play an increasing part in the alteration of the landscape. Moorland farms are realising increasingly higher prices and the capital outlay incurred by the modern farmer in this region will necessitate more intensive methods of husbandry. The suckler-cow industry as it is managed at present is likely to lose ground. Fences are going up on the open downs, land is being improved. Hitherto, the existence of the commons has preserved many of the open moorland areas, but recent legislation may make it possible by the mutual consent of the commoners for the character of the grazing lands to be changed.

Industrial development, the growing resident population and the holiday trade are responsible for a major change in the appearance of the moor by the construction of reservoirs. Cornwall has a high rainfall but the rivers are small with a quick

169

run-off and because of the tourist industry the heaviest demands for water coincide with the period of lowest yield. The policy is, therefore, to construct regulating reservoirs to accumulate large stocks of water to be used to maintain an adequate flow in rivers from which water is extracted for domestic and industrial use. The construction of desalinisation plants has been considered but ruled out because of the cost and the loss of amenity. The building of an estuarial barrage in the Tamar has been lobbied but this suggestion wins no favour either, chiefly on the grounds that such a solution would require prolonged and expensive study and, even if the ecological change of the estuary could be accepted and even if it proved feasible, it would be overtaken by events. The insatiable demand for water dictates a hand-to-mouth policy. The regulating reservoir, therefore, is considered the most practicable answer to the problem and Bodmin Moor with its relatively high altitude, its heavy rainfall and its land of minimal agricultural value, is inevitably regarded as one of the most appropriate gathering grounds. This development offends both the farmer and the conservationist. Although adequate compensation is paid, the affected farms cease to be viable and farmers have to move, some of them for the first time in their lives. Conservationists are also strongly opposed to this development, not only because of the social implications, but also because they regard an artificial sheet of water in a shallow granite valley as a geological monstrosity, for it cannot possibly look like a natural feature as it does in a glaciated Derbyshire valley, where often it occupies the site of a former lake. It is interesting to note that Crowdy Reservoir, which covers a shallow bog on a high table land seems much less of an intrusion than Siblyback in its valley setting.

It can be effectively argued that these are legitimate pressures. The tin, the copper, the wolfram, the china-clay, the granite, the water are needed for the service of man and they cannot be extracted without some loss of amenity. The alternative would seem to be the preservation of the moor for recreational purposes. Preservation, however, is itself a dangerous concept as those who visit the Sussex Downs to the east of the Cuckmere valley are made to realise. In that lovely part of England a large area of downland is the property of the local water board which denies the use of the ground for stock grazing. In the days when these hills belonged to the rabbit and the South-down flock, the open spaces outside the gorse were as smooth as a bowling green and it was a joy to walk on the scented springy turf. Now, nature has taken over and the land is unkempt with rough grass and hidden brambles like a barbed-wire entangle-ment. For aesthetic as well as economic reasons, the moor should continue to be actively farmed.

Tourism is itself one of the most dangerous pressures on the moorland area and in the opinion of many is becoming an embarrassment in the county as a whole. In his inaugural lecture as the newly appointed Director and Professor of Cornish Studies in the University of Exeter, Charles Thomas said in April, 1973: 'The basic problem of the tourist trade—which, let us face it, the vast majority of the people of Cornwall dislike intensely and regard as a poor substitute for a perma-nent industrial provision—is that it poses such a terrifying threat to the physical environment'. There was a time when Cornwall was protected, if 'protected' is the word, by the inadequacy of the trunk roads, the A38, known as 'the longest lane in England' and the A30 which was even narrower. Now the extension of the motorway and the widening of the trunk roads have brought the South West within easy reach of Lon-don and the Midlands. This has greatly benefited Cornwall's principal industry, but there is now real danger of over-production. Many of the Cornish coastal resorts are, in the local idiom, 'as full as can hold' and it has already proved necessary to impose traffic restrictions in narrow, tortuous street systems like that at Polperro. The county council has felt com-pelled to designate certain parts of the coast—about a quarter of it—as 'saturation areas' where no extension of caravan sites or holiday chalet development will be permitted.

THE FUTURE OF THE MOOR

The goal of the holiday-maker has always been the coast and until recent years the moor has received very little attention from the tourist. Indeed, his only knowledge of it has been obtained from brief glimpses of open rolling country as he hurtles along the main trunk road on his way to the coast. Now that the A30 is being developed as a dual carriageway his acquaintance with it will be of even briefer duration. Those who want Bodmin Moor to be left alone may well be grateful for this modern development, but how soon will it be before the planners, desperate to relieve pressure on the coast, start to erect seductive signposts to tempt the tourist onto the moor?

There was actually an abortive attempt to do this in 1971, when the Countryside Commission offered a grant to Cornwall County Council for the setting-up, on an experimental basis, of a holiday motor route in an inland area. Bodmin Moor and its immediate neighbourhood was selected for consideration and a route was planned for the Steering Committee to examine. This committee was representative of a wide range of interests: local landowners, the Cornwall commoners, members of amenity groups, archaeologists, naturalists and professional planners. Except for the planners, who were highly conscious of the fact that the coastal areas were crammed to bursting point every summer, the committee was firmly opposed to the route suggested and, indeed, to any scenic route at all. Faced with this strong body of public opinion the county council abandoned the project.

The opposition to the scenic route scheme was based on such practical considerations as the narrowness of the lanes and the predictable disruption of local traffic, but behind it all was the fear and dislike of the tourist invasion shared by almost all local residents except those who derive their living from it. Perhaps Cornwall has never forgotten that it is a conquered country. Certainly there has been a change in the attitude of the moorland farmer towards the visitor. Sixty years ago he delighted in his all too rare contacts with strangers. He lived in a remote place, often a mile or more from the nearest metalled road, without newspapers, without radio. He ate home-cured bacon, he burned peat, he had no outside human contacts except those provided by the occasional visit to church or chapel or market. His only means of transport was a rough moorland pony on which he scampered about the countryside with his feet almost touching the ground. Now his situation is different. The remote farm-houses are, for the most part, abandoned. The moor farmer lives at the end of a motorable road, he is in contact with the media and his condition is much the same as that of farmers who live in the surrounding villages. The visitor has ceased to be a joy, he is becoming a nuisance. So irascible notices are painted on the farm gates and the Commoners' Association is becoming more belligerent. Walkers and horsemen visit the moor in rapidly increasing numbers and it is natural enough that they are less welcome than they used to be. The conflict of interest between agriculture and tourism is sharpening.

Conservationists are as concerned about the increasing pressures of tourism as the moor farmers. Some of them would like to enter into a conspiracy of silence about the moor. They are like the early visitors who discovered Cornwall in the day when its coves were as empty as the Sutherland coast still is, those who had their favourite beaches and kept quiet about them. They are defending a lost cause. Inevitably the moor will be increasingly used for recreational purposes, not only by the visitor from beyond the Tamar, but also by the local resident from the expanding villages on the moor's edge. But all those who live on or near the moor, whatever their job, whatever their interests, are united in the belief that the sense of peace that the moor conveys is the factor that is most worth fighting for.

Neither the farmer nor the conservationist welcomes any development which encourages large concentrations of people on the moor. The moorland reservoirs provide a case in point. At Siblyback, on a tributary stream which feeds the Fowey, a reservoir of 140 acres was constructed in 1969. On its shores are car-parks, a picnic area and a clubhouse. There are facilities for fishing and sailing. It is more than a sports centre, it is a focal point for people interested in the flora and fauna of the moor and its archaeological remains. Crowdy Reservoir, near Camelford, is also a centre of moorland study. There is much to be said for this sort of development and it can be agreed that it would be uncivilised to surround a regulating reservoir with a fence bristling with 'Keep Out' notices. But it can also be said that as reservoirs proliferate it may be unwise to 'landscape' them and adapt them to organised recreational use. With development of this kind, we may soon arrive at a situation in which Cornwall's wild central area will be reduced to a series of linear parks divided by artificial lakes which, by comparison, will reduce the haunting and beautiful tarn of Dozmary, with its legendary associations, to an insignificant puddle unworthy of notice. The landscape would be conventionalised and stripped of its individuality.

It is perhaps unfortunate that as a result of the reorganisation of local government, the moorland area is divided between two planning authorities. This could well lead to piecemeal planning which might have serious repercussions on the moor as a whole. It could lead to hasty and short-term decisions and to a multiplication of small planning projects which in the long term could do more harm than good. Although it is desirable that each small locality should have a voice in the decisions that are made, an overall policy is needed for the moorland area as a whole. The problem of the moor and the tourist is a difficult one. This is an area where the visitor has no legal right of access except to the network of public roads, a few footpaths and to Roughtor in the north-western corner. Horse-riders and walkers have always moved freely over the area, but they come in greater numbers every year and the time may be near at hand when they will be no longer tolerated.

So planning should be delicate and unobtrusive. A 'honeypot' policy is unacceptable; the rolling downs do not lend themselves to the construction of picnic areas, for the charm of the moor is a matter of tor profile and wide sweeps of open country rather than separate 'beauty spots'. Large assemblies of cars and people will spoil it. There is a need for great care in the positioning and surfacing of parking areas on land adjoining the moorland roads. These should be few in number and small in size. Those who get most satisfaction from the moor are non-gregarious. If you travel around the moor in high summer you will find plenty of people about, but the groups are small and separate. It would, no doubt, be tidier to herd them together and park them prettily, but that is not what they want.

The open nature and narrow confines of the moor are factors that should impose strict limits on almost every planning operation. Caravans, except in small numbers in well screened sites adjacent to farm-houses, are inappropriate; public lavatories, expensive and difficult to maintain in remote places and subject to vandalism, might well be sited in villages and hamlets on and around the moor rather than in open country; direction signs indicating objects of interest should be sparingly used because one can always carry a map; when they are provided they might well follow the ancient tradition of the district and be mounted on rough granite posts. These are small matters, but when we are considering as small an area as the moor we are necessarily concerned with minutiae.

Such a policy seems to be out of step with present-day attitudes. It can be argued, and is argued in some quarters, that those who oppose the development of the moorland area as a holiday centre are adopting a selfish dog-in-the-manger stance. Why should a couple of hundred moor farmers have everything their own way? Why should a few local landowners and local residents impose their will upon the multitudes of people who wish to come? Why should visitors to Cornwall have to queue for deck chairs and waste precious hours in traffic jams when some of the pressure could be relieved by a radical reassessment of the potential of this sizeable open space? Recreational activities are now institutionalised. This is the age of the holiday camp, the packed terraces at the football ground, the sponsored walk and the motor club. And Bodmin Moor is now a national asset. But it can also be argued that the provision of conventional tourist amenities in this highly specialised area would be a totally destructive process; that it would be folly to attempt to popularise the moor for general and indiscriminate use. Democracy is a blessed concept but democracy concerns minorities as well as majorities, minorities who rightly demand to be allowed to enjoy those rare commodities, silence and peace.

Of course we cannot deny access by surrounding Bodmin Moor with a ring fence. The time is soon coming when some moorland areas may have to be preserved. At present the only tor to which the general public have an inalienable right of access is Roughtor. It would be sad indeed if the visitor were cut off from the upper valley of the Delank and the magnificent area of Twelve Men's Moor. And, it is not only the more spectacular tors that are worthy of preservation. We no longer say as Ruskin said over 100 years ago that 'mountains are the beginning and the end of all natural scenery'. Stretches of open down like High Moor, East Moor, Cardinham Moor, Redhill Downs and Craddock Moor reflect the character of the area as much as the high tors. All these areas, with the exception of Roughtor, are privately owned and any restriction of use and extension of rights is likely to prove an expensive and difficult operation. It would be well if some parts of the moor were secured from industrial development and from the erection of fencing, and it would be desirable also to deny access to all forms of transport except the farm vehicles of those who own or rent the land. Preserved areas should be actively farmed for, economic considerations apart, this is the best way of preserving them. The charm of the moor lies in the fact that it is a country which is managed and developed so that men may live.

If it should become possible for some parts of the moor to be dedicated to public use and maintained more or less in their present condition they should be selected, not only for their scenic attraction, but also with regard to their wealth of

176

archaeological sites. Reference was made in an earlier chapter to the investigation of a Bronze Age hut settlement on Stannon Downs. This was undertaken because the site was about to be covered by over-burden from the neighbouring clay works. In one sense no harm has been done. The prehistoric remains were expertly examined and recorded and now they are not destroyed, but preserved under masses of china-clay waste, to be rediscovered, perhaps, in centuries to come. Nevertheless, something has been lost. To the visitor interested in the past the moor is of immense value, because the past is everywhere present.

The moor provides wide scope for a study of animal and plant life. In spite of the pressures upon it the area has remained relatively undisturbed and it becomes increasingly important at a time when so much wild land is being tamed. It is not a primeval area, for man has modified the landscape continuously for more than 4,000 years, but the changes he has wrought have, hitherto, been the result of a slow and gradual process, enabling indigenous animals and plants to adapt themselves to gradually changing circumstances. Violent industrial development or the provision of large-scale tourist facilities would have serious effects not only on the land itself, but on all forms of animal and vegetable life that draw their sustenance from it. The fact that well over a quarter of the moor has been designated a site of special scientific interest is an indication of its importance to the naturalist, and it is highly desirable that this small but varied area should be preserved in its present condition. The interest that it generates would not be appropriately fostered by the setting-up of a series of nature trails. The value of the moor to those interested in its flora and fauna lies in the fact that it is a self-contained entity in which plant and animal life is closely inter-related, in spite of the marked variations of habitat. One can generalise by saying that the plant life of the area is largely conditioned by agricultural use and the acid nature of the soil, and that for animal and bird life the most important factor is the peace and quiet of the neighbourhood.

Land improvement and enclosure would seriously affect the one and large-scale human invasion would change the other.

As we have seen, many of the villages that surround the moor are settlements of great attractiveness. Time cannot stand still and new houses are needed in all these villages, but some of them, perhaps, are growing rather too rapidly for their own good. The Tamar road bridge has turned all south-east Cornwall into commuter country and the old mining hamlets around Caradon are vigorously expanding. This is open country and the new housing estates at Pensilva, Commonmoor and Tremar are visible for miles. Further west, in the richly wooded lowland parts of St Neot, Warleggan, Cardinham and Blisland, development is slower but it is gaining ground. Some of these villages, like many others in Cornwall, are attracting strangers who have come to settle for retirement. This has its advantages. Many of the newcomers are appreciative of the beauty of the area and are actively engaged in the struggle to preserve it, and some of them make a valuable contribution to the life of the local community. In a number of the villages the immigrants constitute a very small minority, so that the life and atmosphere of the place has not been changed, but the influx is continuous and many settlements around the moor may soon have an abnormally high proportion of elderly people. Already in some places this is affecting the school population. The primary schools of the neighbourhood are mostly housed in old buildings badly in need of modernisation or replacement. This could well lead to the closure of some of them and the local authority would be unlikely to build new schools in areas where the school population is declining. This would impoverish the village community, subjecting young children to long daily journeys and cutting them off from rural life. The problem of the holiday cottage which stands empty for most of the year is another disquieting modern feature.

The stranger coming to Bodmin Moor might well spare a few minutes to turn aside to the churchyard at Temple in the heart of the moor. The church, a simple late Victorian building, has no distinction and the churchyard itself is an unkempt area very little different from the moorland that surrounds it. But an examination of the small collection of gravestones reveals that those whose bodies lie there have been gathered in from different parts of the country. They have come home. It is a small piece of evidence of the peculiar fascination this moorland area exerts over those who belong to it. Its continued development should be along the lines of gradual organic change and not as the result of violent transformation. This compelling country can preserve its quality only if its integrity is respected and only if planners are sensitive to its own peculiar needs.

PRINCIPAL ANTIQUITIES

(Grid references are to sheet 186 of the One-Inch Ordnance Survey Map and Sheets 200 and 201 of the 1:50,000 metric maps)

ANCIENT BRIDGES	Berriow (274755)
	Key Bridge (099738)
	Panters Bridge (160680)
	Treverbyn (206674)
BARROWS	Alex Tor (117786)
(a selection)	Carey Tor (231770)
	Emblance Downs (130770)
	Summit of Brown Gelly (195725)
	Summit of Buttern Hill (175816)
	Summit of Carburrow (157708)
CHAMBER TOMB	Trethevy Quoit (259688)
CLAPPER BRIDGES	Bedrawle (132765)
	Bradford (129754)
	Butter's Tor (150786)
	Delphy (115759)
CROSSES AND INSCRIBED STONES	Craddock Moor (256705)
	Fourholes Cross (171749)
	King Doniert's Stone (236688)
	Middlemoor Cross (125793)
	Welltown, Cardinham (136678)
ENCLOSURES AND HILL FORTS	Allabury (258769)
	Berry Down (195688)
	Bray Down (191825)
	Bury Castle (135696)
	The Crowpound (175677)
	King Arthur's Hall (130777)
	Roughtor (145810)
	Stowe's Pound (257726)

PRINCIPAL ANTIQUITIES

HOLY WELLS

Cardinham (126693)
St Breward (092768)
St Cleer (249684)
St Clether (202846)
St Neot (181681)

HUT SETTLEMENTS
(a selection)

Blacktor Downs (157735)
Browngelly Downs (202727)
Kerrow Downs (115750)
Leskernick Hill (184800)
Roughtor Ford (145810)

MESOLITHIC FLINT SITE

Dozmary Pool (197745)

NEOLITHIC HENGE

Stripple Stones (143752)

STONE CIRCLES

Craddock Moor (249718)
Fernacre (145800)
Goodaver (210752)
The Hurlers (258715)
Leaze (137775) and (137772)
Nine Stones (236781)
Stannon (127800)
Trippet Stones (131750)

BIBLIOGRAPHY

Alcock, Leslie. *Arthur's Britain* (Middlesex, 1971, 1973)

Balchin, W. G. V. *Cornwall—The Making of the English Landscape* (1954)

Baring-Gould, S. *A Book of Cornwall* (1899)

Barton, D. B. *The Mines and Mineral Railways of East Cornwall and West Devon* (Truro Bookshop, 1964)

Barton, R. M. *An Introduction to the Geology of Cornwall* (Truro Bookshop, 1964)

——. *A History of the Cornish China-clay Industry* (Truro, 1966)

Burrows, R. *The Naturalist in Devon and Cornwall* (Newton Abbot, 1971)

Carew, Richard. *The Survey of Cornwall—1602*, ed. F. E. Halliday (Bath, 1970)

Chambers, E. K. *Arthur of Britain* (1927, 1966)

Chesher, V. M. and F. J. *The Cornishman's House* (Truro, 1968)

Chope, R. Pearse (ed.) *Early Tours in Devon and Cornwall* (Newton Abbot, 1967)

Coate, Mary. *Cornwall in the Great Civil War and Interregnum* (Oxford, 1933)

Doble, G. H. *St Neot, Abbot and Confessor*, Cornish saints series (Exeter, 1929)

——. *Saint Samson in Cornwall*, Cornish saints series (Exeter, 1935)

du Maurier, Daphne. *Vanishing Cornwall* (1966, 1972)

Elliott-Binns, L. E. *Medieval Cornwall* (1955)

Fox, Aileen. *South West England* (1964)

Hamilton Jenkin, A. K. *Around Liskeard*, Mines and Miners of Cornwall series XII (Truro Bookshop, 1966)

——. *Wadebridge, Camelford, Bude*, Mines and Miners of Cornwall series XVI (Federation of Old Cornwall Societies, 1970)

Hedgeland, J. P. *A Description of the Decorations Recently Made to the Church of St Neot in Cornwall* (privately printed, 1830)

Hencken, H. O'N. *The Archaeology of Cornwall and Scilly* (1932)

Henderson, C. *The Cornish Church Guide* (1928; Truro, 1965)

Henderson, C. *Essays in Cornish History* (Oxford, 1935; Truro, 1963)
Henderson, C. and Coates, H. *Old Cornish Bridges and Streams* (1928; Truro, 1972)
Hind, G. Lewis. *Days in Cornwall* (1907)
Hockin, J. R. A. *Walking in Cornwall* (1936)
Hoskins, W. G. and Stamp, L. D. *The Common Lands of England and Wales* (1963)
Lane-Davies, A. *Holy Wells of Cornwall* (Federation of Old Cornwall Societies, 1970)
Latham, Bryan. *Trebartha, the House by the Stream* (1971)
Leigh, Margaret. *Harvest of the Moor* (1937)
Maclean, Sir John. *History of Trigg Minor* (Bodmin, 1873)
Malim, J. W. *The Bodmin Moors* (1936)
Mere, R. *Wildlife in Cornwall* (Truro, 1970)
Michell, James. *Parochial History of St Neot's in Cornwall* (Bodmin, 1833)
Munn, P. *Bodmin Moor* (Bodmin, 1972)
Murray's Handbook for Devon and Cornwall (1859; repr Newton Abbot, 1971)
Norden, John. *Description of Cornwall* (1728; repr Newcastle, 1966)
One-inch Ordnance Survey (1st ed) sheets 89 and 90 (repr Newton Abbot, 1969)
Paton, J. A. *Wild Flowers in Cornwall* (Truro, 1968)
Pearce, John. *The Wesleys in Cornwall* (Truro, 1964)
Pevsner, N. *Cornwall: The Buildings of England* (Middlesex, 1951)
Quiller-Couch, M. and L. *Ancient and Holy Wells of Cornwall* (1894)
Rowe, John. *Cornwall in the Age of the Industrial Revolution* (Liverpool, 1953)
Rowse, A. L. *Tudor Cornwall* (1941, 1969)
Rushforth, G. McN. 'The Windows of the Church of St Neot, Cornwall', *Transactions of the Exeter Diocesan Architectural and Archaeological Society*, XV (1937)
Shorter, Ravenhill and Gregory. *South West England* (1969)
Todd, A. C. and Laws, P. *Industrial Archaeology of Cornwall* (Newton Abbot, 1972)
Woolf, Charles. *An Introduction to the Archaeology of Cornwall* (Truro, 1970)

ACKNOWLEDGEMENTS

I am greatly indebted to Carolyn Brewster, Research Fellow of the Institute of Cornish Studies, for providing the short article on the vegetational characteristics of Bodmin Moor. The illustrations are the work of Charles Woolf of Newquay, the late Phillip Duncan of St Neot and my son Roger. Colonel W. E. Almond furnished me with useful information about the fauna of the moor and the Reverend W. A. Kneebone, formerly vicar of Altarnun, supplemented my knowledge of that great moorland parish. S. J. Bolitho, T. Burgess and A. R. Hanbury-Tenison gave me much help in the preparation of the section on farming practice and the management of the commons. I am grateful to the captain of the Park Clayworks and to the manager and foreman of the Delank Granite Quarry. My thanks are also due to W. A. Pascoe for showing me round the slate caverns at Carnglaze. I owe a special debt of gratitude to the late Dennis Jeffery, for typing the manuscript. My wife was responsible not only for causing me to think I now understand something of the complicated geology and geomorphology of the area, but also for encouraging me during the long period of the book's gestation.

INDEX

INDEX

INDEX

St Neot—cont.
164; slate quarries, 163; tourism, 164
Samson, St, 86
Scenic route, 172
Schools, 178
Scribble Downs, 42
Shallow Water Common, 12, 49, 105
Sharp Tor, 16, 50, 52, 137
Showery Tor, 14, 48
Site of Special Scientific Interest, 177
Slates, 39
Slaughter Bridge, 80
Smallacoombe Downs, 33
Snipe, 19
Spoure Family, 134
Staniforth, Thomas, 45
Stannaries, 19
Stanning Hill, 42, 159
Stannon, 118, 120
Stannon Down, 73, 177
Stone Circles: Craddock Moor, 66;
    Fernacre, 66, 69; Goodaver, 9, 66;
    Hurlers, the, 45, 65; Leaze, 66; Nine
    Stones, 66; Stannon, 66, 69, 120;
    Trippet Stones, 66, 67
Stowe's Hill, 16, 44, 45, 52
Stowe's Pound, 52, 77, 54
Stripple Stones, 62
Suckler cow industry, 115, 169
Swaling, 30, 31

Temple, 20, 26, 84, 87, 128, 145–6, 178
Thomas, Professor Charles, 171

Tolborough (or Tober) Tor, 28, 49
Tolkien, J. R. R., 148
Tors, 40
Tourism, 123, 164, 171
Trebartha, 16, 52, 135
Tregarrick Tor, 56, 57
Tregeagle, John, 27, 82
Tregulland, 69
Tremar, 56, 136, 137
Trenant, 19, 150
Trengoffe, 139, 160
Treslea Downs, 65
Treswallock Downs, 65
Trethevy Quoit, 63–4
Treverbyn Bridge, 16, 95
Trevillians Gate, 14, 47
Trewint, 26, 133
Trewortha Tor, 40, 42, 44, 50, 80, 105
Trezibbet, 26
Turpinke Acts, 25, 144
Twelve Men's Moor, 50, 176

Upton Cross, 56
Uranium, 98

Valley Truckle, 131

Warleggan, 16, 139–40
Wenmouth Cross, 26
Wesley, John, 134
Whinchat, 29
Witheybrook, 16, 42, 50
Wolfram, 14, 98, 170